T0354297

THE HUMAN SPIRIT, STORIES FROM THE HEART

By Larry Welch

Order this book online at www.trafford.com
or email orders@trafford.com

Most Trafford titles are also available at major online book retailers.

Print information available on the last page.

ISBN: 978-1-4269-1597-0 (sc)

Trafford rev. 06/28/18

 www.trafford.com

North America & international
toll-free: 1 888 232 4444 (USA & Canada)
fax: 812 355 4082

**For my late father,
Lawrence Nelson Welch, Sr.,
(1921-2005),
Always with me**

What people are saying about
The Human Spirit

Larry has given the world a great gift in collecting these inspiring experiences for his book. Through the magic of words, he leads the reader on journeys around the world, introducing us to fascinating people of goodwill, sharing their inspiring stories, and giving unique insight into their cultures. It is heartwarming to know that Larry has found a common goodness in so many unusual encounters, sometimes beginning with just an exchange of smiles. Each story could stand alone in serving readers a daily dose of inspiration like a vitamin to energize the soul. Read as a whole, each exemplary experience reinforces the message of the others. Thanks, Larry, for this collection of optimistic stories about our wonderful human family. Jean Spike, Delaware, Ohio, USA*

At last, Larry has compiled his unique experiences into one volume. This wonderful book reaches out to readers who love snippets and vignettes as well as touching stories about travel and the human spirit. His well-written prose paints exquisite pictures of our humanity. "The Human Spirit, Stories from the Heart" will definitely bring CHEER to readers. The spirit of compassion, healing, endurance, endearment and the entertaining quality of our relationships is alive and well in this extremely interesting book. After reading it cover-to-cover, I recommend it to everyone who loves the human spirit. Ernest Chen, entrepreneur, author, professional speaker, Singapore

I've enjoyed reading Larry's book. It is so refreshing and enlightening as he promotes a generosity in giving of the human spirit. Wherever he travels he learns about people, then taking his experiences, good or bad, and making them into a positive

lesson in living. The insights in this book make you re-evaluate the way you should live and definitely gives you a more positive outlook on life! Anna Tjoumas, elementary school teacher and librarian, Manassas, Virginia, USA

I have been reading Larry's "On the Run" articles for years, often sending them to friends who found the human interest to be an enriching experience. This book is just as enjoyable.... sometimes evoking laughter, sometimes tears as he details parts of his life's journey. He constantly challenges us to introspection and self analysis....and that's a good thing! Karen Edwards, Hilton Head, South Carolina, USA

The earth is a broad expanse with positive people not easily brought together. To meet and know someone like Larry who inspires us to sincere optimism is a marvelous experience. Through the power of words, Larry uses the lives of others to stimulate readers to a higher level of thinking. Through his experiences we learn that people aren't perfect, things don't always go as smoothly as we'd like, and the world is not all peace and happiness. Nevertheless, there are happy endings for those who keep chasing a hope and dream. Larry's love, open-mindedness, richly felt humanity, powers of observation and beautiful words fill us with the power of life. I hope one day I can touch the heart of others the way this man does in his writing. Ivory Chang, Chinese teacher, Suankularb Wittayalai Rangsit School, Phanumthini, Thailand

The Somaly Mam Foundation

All royalties for *The Human Spirit, Stories from the Heart* are being donated to The Somaly Mam Foundation, a nonprofit public charity committed to ending slavery. With the vision and leadership of world renowned Cambodian activist, Somaly Mam, the foundation focuses on eradicating the root of human trafficking, exemplifying a global vision and dedication that will allow its work in the United States and Southeast Asia to expand to other countries around the world.

For more information on The Somaly Mam Foundation visit www.somaly.org. Thank you for your support!

Profits from sexual slavery are estimated to be $7-12 billion per year. United Nations Office of Drugs and Crime

2-4 million young women and girls will be sold into prostitution in the next 12 months...

Human trafficking is the second-largest organized crime in the world. It has become a bigger business than drug trafficking generating more than $9.5 billion a year. US State Department

Many of these children are sold into sexual slavery for as little as $10 and some as young as 5. Anderson Cooper 360

Human trafficking victims are subjected to rape, torture, forced abortions, starvation, and threats to family members. UNICEF

About the Author

Larry Welch resides in Thailand where he operates the Full Moon Rubber Plantation at Nakhon Phanom and teaches English at the Suankularb Wittayalai Rangsit School at Phanumthini, a suburb and province north of Bangkok. In his day-to-day routine he teaches 500 students a week in grades 7 through 12. Although only a second year teacher, it is his belief that it's impossible to have a bad day when surrounded by that much good-natured humanity.

In 1995 and again in 1999, he was selected as Toastmaster of the Year for the District of Columbia, Northern Virginia and Southern Maryland. In 1996, he became the first recipient of the National Race for the Cure Volunteer of the Year Award; and he was presented the 1997 Jill Ireland Award for Voluntarism by The Susan G. Komen Breast Cancer Foundation in Dallas, Texas. In 1998 and again in 2002, the Naval Criminal Investigative Service presented him a Department of the Navy Meritorious Civilian Service Award for his leadership in community service and contributions to the agency mission. Toastmasters International has also recognized him as their Club President of the Year and Division Governor of the Year.

An avid reader and learner, in 1995, he earned a Bachelor of Science degree (management) from University College, University of Maryland, after attending night school for nine years.

In 1984, he retired from the Navy as a Lieutenant (Limited Duty-Cryptology). Before a second retirement with the US Naval Criminal Investigative Service in 2007, he was employed as a civilian security specialist in Singapore performing vulnerability assessments at seaports and airfields in Asia and the South Pacific.

For the past ten years he has authored electronic newsletters, *Briefly Brinker* and *On the run...*, which reflect a street-smart philosophy on the places he visits and people he meets--along with ideas on how we can be our best.

He is author of *Mary Virginia, A Father's Story*; and *Quotations for Positive People, And Those Who Would Like to Be*.

Larry can be reached by e-mail at <u>lnwelch@aol.com</u>.

Prologue

The 96 vignettes in *Stories from the Heart* first appeared in *Briefly Brinker* or *On the run...* during 1998-2003. I created these two electronic newsletters to recognize achievement, challenge readers to adopt change, and promote personal growth. Later, *On the run...* evolved into a reflection of my experiences living in Singapore and Thailand.

These materials are reproduced in book form to provide a collection of thoughts for readers of today's *On the run...* as well as to be a permanent reference for my family, friends, and new readers.

The stories are about all kinds of people from young to old, Americans and those who were born and always lived in foreign lands. Readers will be happy to learn more about the good hearts in this world, how strong and generous we can be in our compassion, and learn a little about greed. It's not always easy being who we are, life is complicated with lots of moving parts, but the more we see faith, hope and optimism reflected in those around us, the more confident we can be in our own journey.

There is no real theme to this collection, which has captured human spirits in homelessness, some with life threatening diseases, children looking at the world through the eyes of innocence, and senior citizens living pretty good lives. Readers will get a glimpse into the world of foreigners and, if anything, I hope you will turn the last page over with a sense that we really are one human family with brothers and sisters in every nation, in every religion, and in every color of skin.

Table of Contents

2001

2002

2003

Resolutions for 1999

We are approaching an extraordinary opportunity to do well in our own lives and those of others. Yes, it's time for New Year's Resolutions again! If there is anyone who can't think of a thing they would like to adopt as a resolution, please consult my list. I've put in easy things for those less resolute, romantic thoughts for the dreamers, practical ideas of those who take life too seriously and fun ideas for clowns or those who would like to be. At any rate, I hope you enjoy this offering. There is a little of you and a little of me in each and something for most moods. Remember, resolutions can be made anytime and the most pronounced good comes when they are not broken:Adopt a charity, applaud achievement, be brave, be a hero, be committed, be daring, be excited, be fair-minded, be generous, be good, be honest, be humane, be part of the solution, be positive, be proud of your heritage, be yourself, become a little eccentric, become a mentor, become involved, become your own best friend, believe in miracles, break paradigms, brush and floss daily, buy a book (read it!), call your mother, celebrate someone or something every day, create a good road map for your life's journey, decide not to bungee jump! Develop balance, develop trust, devote yourself to one sunset, discover classical music, discover humor, discover nature, do a very good deed, do something unexpected, don't chew tobacco, don't start barroom brawls you can't finish, don't tolerate child abuse, drive safely, dwell on possibilities, eat your vegetables, embrace and care for the elderly, embrace people, embrace the wonders of your world, establish short and long term goals, exercise more, extend yourself for foreigners, fall in love, feed the birds, feed the hungry, fill your head with positive thoughts, fill your life with purpose and meaning, find a hobby, find yourself, follow a dream, follow through with everything, forgive, fulfill your great potential, get a mentor, get a physical, get off the treadmill, get serious about self-improvement, giggle more, give more applause, give more than expected, give someone a boost, give someone a hand, give thanks, go on a balloon ride, go canoeing, go to the circus, go on a diet, go out two nights a week, go to a movie, help a neighbor, hug a child, join the clean plate club, join the warm handshake club, keep learning new things, keep things in perspective, keep your head high, laugh more, lead a parade, learn about life, learn something from one sunrise, learn to like spiders, let a smile be your umbrella, light a candle, limit yourself to two six packs a day, listen more, live it up, love your pet, lower your cholesterol, lower your expectations of others, make a list of 101 things you like, make a new friend, make up with your enemy, make eye contact more, make someone happy every day, plant four leaf clovers, practice charisma, practice creativity, preserve your motivation, put on your thinking cap, raise expectations for yourself, reach up-reach out, recycle, reflect on potential solutions, reflect on your greatness, ride a bicycle, ride a merry-go-round, practice being silly now and then, pray for the parents of terminally ill children, protect your child, grandchild, or a neighborhood munchkin, save for a rainy day, say *yes*, seek improvement—not perfection, see the world through the eyes of a child, see worth through the eyes of a clown, see the world through the eyes of the elderly, send someone flowers, show your colors, simplify your life, sit on a park bench 30 minutes a week, slay the dragon of mistrust, sleep in now and then, slow down—speed up (take your choice), smile more, start more conversations, start a daily journal, start believing, stop being afraid of the dark, stop whining, stretch yourself, support someone special, surround yourself with successful people, surprise yourself, take a night class, take a walk, take a vacation, take charge, take up where someone else left off, talk less, turn over a new leaf, use it up—wear it out—make it do, use your noodle more, use your seat belt, visit a cemetery, visit Denver, visit a library, visit a museum, visit a nursing home, visit the zoo, visit your dentist cheerfully, volunteer, volunteer as an organ donor, vow to make life a fun experience, walk in the rain, watch less television, wish upon a star for someone's happiness, write a poem, write a short story.

Dreams, Goals, and a Plan

One evening in January, I met Gary Curtis at the intersection of 5th and New York Avenue, NW, in Washington, DC. The neighborhood isn't pretty there. Streets are littered and untrimmed shrubbery is refuge to wayward paper and plastic that flutters in winter winds.

The season's grayness darkened the scene as I watched a line of homeless men and women who were receiving a handout from our mobile food van. Gary, a tall young man, had been through the line and stood a few feet away. He asked me where I came from and how he could also help feed homeless people. His request was unusual. In five years of helping street people with food, no one else had ever asked me that question.

I gave him the address of our sponsor, Martha's Table, and for a few minutes we spoke quietly about the weather, people, and homelessness. Gary finally disclosed that four months earlier, he had owned a car, lived in a house, and worked at a job, but that alcohol and drugs had changed his life for the worse.

He went on to relate that a local minister was helping him with a resume, interview skills, and clothes. Gary was excited about his dreams, goals and plans for the future. He confidently predicted a better life, assured me he'd soon be working and that one of his immediate goals really was to help the homeless through Martha's Table.

He told me his new life would be much different than the past. Since that day, it was January 19, 1999, I have thought of Gary often. I think of him in the sense of Maryland's Harriet Tubman who, once escaping slavery herself, returned 19 times to help others escape. Gary's approach also illustrates that regardless of life's position, we must all have dreams, goals, and a plan to move us. I was fortunate to have had that conversation and thought you'd like to know about it.

Choices, Decisions and Directions

Last week I was fortunate to meet two people that reminded me of how important it is to make good choices early in life.

On April 9, I met Jessica Carlson, not her real name by the way. Jessica is a 40-year old inmate at the Fairfax County Jail. In our conversation, she remorsefully recounted a 27-year courtship with heroin, 53 arrests, and estrangement from her four children. It's not easy swallowing pride; however, she painfully disclosed mistakes, misjudgments, and wrong choices. Other inmates who also heard Jessica's story were spellbound by her candor and eloquence.

Listening to her story I felt terrible to see this beautiful woman at such a low point in her life.

The following morning, I had a meeting that contrasted with the one with Jessica. This time I met Kim Roman. As a coincidence, Kim is also 40-years old. She is a single mom with two young children, head of a business she created, and possesses phenomenal community spiritedness. Kim also has an addiction—it's a passion to become the best she can for her kids, career and community. I listened as she explained her background and reasons for wanting to improve her life. Inwardly, I marveled at her positive attitude and wondered why all of us can't be as motivated.

Later, I reflected on the two women, both radiant in the beauty of their personalities, but with contrasting accomplishments. The difference was in choices that they had made year's earlier. While Jessica may have decided to experiment with drugs, Kim was probably doing extra effort to get an A in school. Who knows and at this point it's not terribly important. Today's result is what matters now.

What these two charismatic people teach us is that the decisions of today, even small ones, will be our fortune. Whether the fortune is a bounty or bust depends on the quality of our choices.

Nellie Eastwood

Unless you live in the vicinity of Herndon, Virginia, or chance upon the *Herndon Observer* newspaper for Mar 5, you wouldn't know that Nellie Eastwood had passed. She was 100-years old and not wealthy so there were no large bequests to endow a college or hospital. She wasn't famous, hadn't invented anything, and wasn't a movie star. But when I read her obituary, her legacy became clear.

Her daughter was quoted as saying: *Everyone that met her loved her.* Dr. Richard Prassel, her minister said: *She is greatly loved, widely respected, and viewed as a spiritual giant.*

I especially liked Sally Myers comment: *She was always kind, always cheerful, always had a smile on her face...she's one of the ones who touched my heart, and she'll be greatly missed.*

Nellie was the oldest member of her church and retirement community. She left a wonderful legacy driven by a positive personality.

She personally contributed to those around her. Kind words, a smile, a gentle manner were trademarks. Nellie is gone, but she has left us things to ponder. What are we willing to do now to make the world better for those around us? How do we want to be remembered?

In their book, *Yes, You Can*, Sam Deep and Lyle Sussman wrote: *A recent study of people over the age of ninety-five reported that one of their greatest regrets was their failure to leave behind something of worth to humanity.*

Deep and Sussman then offered suggestions on things we can all do for our legacy. Their thoughts were to speak out against social ills, moral evils, and human suffering. Be a gadfly for good. Will your vital organs to an organ bank. Develop teaching skills. Look for opportunities in your organization to train new employees so that they can advance their careers, feel better about themselves, and accomplish more for the customers of the organization. Volunteer to work with young people at your school, church, or synagogue. Get involved with other organizations, such as the Scouts, that benefit the adults of tomorrow. Be a positive role model to the children in your life.

To this list I would add smile more, make eye contact with everyone, reach out to people, make connections with others, shake hands more, talk to strangers, treat everyone you meet as though they are the most important person in the world, and lastly, be like Nellie Eastwood, touch hearts in your own unique way.

Catherine's Story

On April 20, 1999, the Komen National Race for the Cure celebrated 10 great years of giving to the Washington community. To make the occasion special, the great Hall at the Library of Congress was used for an extraordinary program featuring masters-of-ceremonies Jane Pauley and Stone Phillips from *Dateline NBC*; Doreen Getzler, WRC-TV; and Randy Martin, WASH-FM Radio.

Founder of The Komen Foundation, Nancy Brinker; Senator Trent Lott; The Honorable and Mrs. Dan Quayle and a host of political personalities were there along with a contingent of National Football League players.

Catherine Anthony was also on the program. She and three of her breast cancer survivor sisters had been selected to tell their breast cancer stories in a series of public service announcements that were scheduled to appear later on WRC-TV. Catherine received a dozen pink roses from the NFL players as a part of being introduced for this special honor.

My own great experience was visiting with her before escorting her to the stage. We talked candidly about breast cancer. In her case, she had gone into remission simply to have the cancer return and metastasize. It meant a lot to me in meeting Catherine. She put my life back into a more healthy perspective again. I think we all need to be reminded frequently about what's important.

At 40ish, Catherine has every reason to live and with the help of God, continuing medical breakthroughs and her own positive attitude she will experience a long and fruitful life. Rather than a heroine who is fighting hard for her life, she prefers to be known as a woman with determination. Catherine is determined; it shows in her demeanor which is also good humored and optimistic. Everyday a few people are faced with bad situations that have no good choices, some understandably fall apart; others model inner strength that inspires. Through the power she possesses Catherine has the key that fits life's door to success in any endeavor. We should all rejoice for our Catherine's as they light paths that are darkened by fear and self doubt.

The Great Escape

Everyone should have adventures in their life. Whether 7 or 79, life's greatest and most memorable moments are spent with the rush of adrenalin. Anxiety, fear, and suspense in small doses are good defenses to the ho-hum of living a safe, secure life.

If you haven't had a good adventure lately, I will share one that was recently undertaken by my daughter, Mary Virginia.

At 2:35 p.m., Wednesday, July 14, 1999, Mary escaped from KinderCare in Herndon, Va. Waiting for an opportune moment in the outdoor exercise area, she scaled a four-foot fence and slipped away, sometimes running, the three blocks to her home. There she climbed a six-foot privacy fence to attempt entrance to her house through a rear door or window. Finding entry difficult, she retreated back over the privacy fence to execute her backup plan—hanging out at the neighborhood playground. En route she was spotted by the KinderCare police and crawled underneath a parked pick-up truck to elude pursuers. It was futile.

Apprehended and under interrogation she disclosed that she escaped to prove the point that the KinderCare staff neither cares about kids nor watches them very well. Her punishment was lost privileges—no King's Dominion trip on July 15. Mary is four feet tall, weighs 55 pounds, and is 7-years old. She also watches Disney movies where the kids ultimately triumph, often over blundering adults.

In this situation, she was inspired to creative heroics to prove a point. Mary gave herself and the KinderCare staff a massive dose of anxiety, fear, and suspense. Fortunately, no one was harmed and some good may have actually been achieved. My little girl was sufficiently frightened that she promised never to attempt another escape, the KinderCare staff will be more alert and caring in the future, and I was again reminded about how creative children can be.

Attitude Indicators

It was during the ground school portion of my flight training that I initially learned about one of the most important aircraft systems, the Attitude Indicator. Because we are surrounded by attitudes every day, I thought it ironic that an airplane would have an instrument dedicated to that purpose.

The textbook explanation of an Attitude Indicator says, *it is a vacuum-powered instrument, which senses pitching and rolling movements about the airplane's lateral and longitudinal axes.*

In other words, it indicates levels of bank, descent and climb. When you think about it, people have Attitude Indicators, too. We see them all the time. Attitudes are reflected in the way we respond to our environment. In people, I see positive Attitude Indicators as maintaining eye contact; a warm smile; friendly handshake; energetic, poised and purposeful strides; the willingness to start conversations; sitting in the front row at school or church; and bravely saying *yes* to challenges and opportunities.

Where there are positive attitudes, people are ascending on a good course that is harmonious, happy, productive and satisfying. Conversely, negative attitudes have their indicators, which are just as obvious. My questions for you: *What do your Attitude Indicators say about you? Are you positive? Can you adjust your course to be more positive?*

Optimism Cures

In *Mastery and Mirth* (Jan 30, '00), Dr. Terry Paulson published an enlightening view of optimism. If you like life's sunny side, you'll enjoy his comments:

Charles Carver, in his study of women newly diagnosed with breast cancer found a key difference between optimists and pessimists. Optimists, far from protecting their fragile vision of the world, confront trouble head-on, while it is pessimists who bury their heads in the sand of denial. Optimists were more likely to acknowledge the seriousness of the disease, experienced less distress and took more active steps to cope with it. Pessimism was associated with denial and a giving up response. Optimism was associated with positive reframing the situation, with women believing, "This is not going to go away, so let me make the best of it I can."

Dr. Paulson continued, *the best change agents are optimists. There is no Pollyanna thinking; they believe in real obstacles and the importance of real hard work to overcome them. Rather than avoid problems, they know that with a track record of overcoming past problems, they are likely to find a way to do it again. Leaders need to cultivate stories that capture their team's heroic efforts from the past. Don't be afraid of high goals or talking about past frustrations. When you can, pick people on your team who have a history of "can* do." *Victims tend to look for people and problems to blame. Victors are ready to persist until they find a way. Pessimism and optimism are both contagious. Which attitude do you want to spread?*

In experiences with a variety of organizations and team leaders, I have noted again and again that those people who float to the top of life's great ocean are optimists. They are the positive thinkers who find solutions, create synergy, and nurture harmony. Every day we make important choices, some simple, others more difficult. One choice that we should all conscientiously make until it becomes a habit is to be optimistic. This includes believing in our own abilities, trusting those around us, and having faith that the future will be more satisfying than the past.

Optimism isn't something that comes in the genes; it's a learned trait of people who make choices in lifestyle. What happens to the people who don't float to the surface in life's great ocean? I'll answer that with a question: How long can you hold your breath underwater before you drown? To echo Dr. Paulson, *Optimism and pessimism are both contagious. What attitude do you want to spread?*

An Old Man - The Right Attitude

My grandfather, William Clay Aper, died 35 years ago. Called Will by my grandmother and Bill by his friends, he was a farmer with a peculiar way that I never understood until in recent years.

The patriarch of a 159-acre farm in Southeastern Michigan, he oversaw rolling hills, a pleasant stream, woods, and fields that supplied sustenance for chickens, cows, crows, ducks, horses, mice, pigs, and sheep. There was a large apple orchard, peach trees, and enormous walnut trees that broke the landscape along with a 100-year old farmhouse and barns, coops and sheds for animals, implements and grain storage.

Oddly, my grandfather never progressed much farther than horse and buggy. Most old timers moved to the Model T Ford and beyond, not my granddad. Except for a Minneapolis-Moline tractor and hitching rides with people who drove cars, he stuck with horses until the end. I always thought this a bit strange, but then as a boy it wasn't my place to question, I was there to watch and wonder.

Grandpa was simple in other ways, too. He possessed spontaneous humor and a tendency to laugh often, besides laughter and a playful spirit; he took life in stride, but at his own pace.

Animal husbandry is not an occupation for timid souls, there was extremely hard work in bitter cold and summers that were an inferno but to counterbalance exertion, there was rest. Sundays were always a day to rejuvenate. This was often done in the company of aunts, uncles and cousins who came from all points of the compass to enjoy a day relaxing on the farm.

Adults found re-creation with conversation, horseshoes, croquet, card games, and chasing after kids.

I was recently reminded of my grandfather while reading the article, *Stop the Week*, which appeared in *Reader's Digest* (Nov '99). An essay on simplicity, writer Wayne Muller suggested that in the relentless busyness of modern life, we have lost the rhythm between action and rest which has led to a universal refrain, *I am so busy.*

Muller continued, *We say this to one another as if our exhaustion were a trophy, our ability to withstand stress a mark of character.... to be unavailable to our friends and family, to be unable to find time for the sunset (or even to know the sun has set), to whiz through our obligations without time for a single mindful breath – this has become the model for a successful life.*

He also explained that the more life speeds up, the more we feel weary, overwhelmed, and lost until the whole experience of being alive begins to melt into one enormous obligation.

Although my grandfather was an odd duck in adapting to technology, his attitude and lifestyle were in keeping with the simple pleasures that made him happy and that's what life should be about. If he had a formula for living, I think it would be balancing personal and professional obligations with days filled with humor, peace and joy. Young or old, man or woman, having the right attitude on living should be a conscientious endeavor that we all reevaluate from time-to-time. I am sure that my grandfather would gladly take time to smile and nod in agreement.

The Blue Blanket

As a toddler, I carefully balanced my steps dragging a blue baby blanket. Kids still do that, adults drag around security in a different form.

In my case, at age 18 months, in carefully climbing out of my crib, I got to the top rung, fell overboard and broke my arm. The next week, arm in a cast, I reenacted the exploit without falling over the side. I made it 20-feet and fell down a flight of stairs. And so it goes with security blankets.

As we get to be 4-5 years old, we often replace our blankets, teddy bears and baby dolls for a sense of security that isn't as apparent. We hide behind charm, a smile, shyness, our parents, older brothers and sisters, classmates, spouses, coworkers, excuses, negative thoughts, and fear.

Our adventurous spirits fade, experimentation gives way to comfortable routines. We're afraid of change and the potential for growth to comfortable routines. We're afraid of change and the potential for growth because of failure. There are security blankets everywhere, we just can't see them. What does your security blanket look like? Is it blue, pink or striped?

I could feel like a failure because so many important things that I've tried haven't worked well. I lost a first marriage and now a second; have not yet used my business degree to best advantage or finished a first book effort or requirements for a private pilot's license and to top that off I keep procrastinating on learning a foreign language and taking music lessons.

However, my successes have been humdingers. Through immersing myself in life, I've learned humility, found the best friendships on planet earth, improved my values, become braver, reached maturity, and developed a stronger sense of social responsibility. My morals are better, vision more clear, and I am excited about today and tomorrow.

Who I am today and will be tomorrow is now more important than who I was yesterday. I think about my blue blanket when I see people holding back from their best destiny. Many are hiding behind busyness, laziness, and an unwillingness to create challenges for improvement.

Some of my friends are 50-years old and done; others are much younger but share a common fate. They can't progress because they are totally enveloped in imaginary security blankets. Do you have one? Are you proud of it? The point is that you can let fear smother you or you can breathe deeply, experiment, learn and grow. It's your life, you're responsible. Hang on to your blue blanket or let it go, life is filled with important choices—try not to fall down a flight a stairs as one of them.

To Infinity and Beyond

Because of my 7-year old daughter Mary, I am privileged to have experiences which often lead to unexpected revelations. The life and culture of children isn't really much different from the adult stuff. An example of the adult-child similarity is embodied in Buzz Lightyear, star of the wonderful movie, *Toy Story*, and its sequel.

Buzz starts the film filled with confidence in the belief that he's a space ranger on a mission to save the universe from evil. Attired in a state-of-the-art space suit, he believes he can fly. During the movie, we see Buzz actually muddle through a flight of sorts primarily on the faith that he can do it. Later he learns that he's ... *just a toy.*

Space Ranger Lightyear loses interest in life, his self-image shattered. I felt badly for him. He was on an extraordinary mission; saving the universe is not a responsibility for the timid. His personality and character were superb; he was buoyant with optimism and confidence.

Fortunately, through the support of Sheriff Woody, he learned that he had considerable talent as a toy and could actually accomplish remarkable feats. Kids, toys, movies, life...all teaching points to help us appreciate the value of believing in ourselves AND helping others to define their mission, talent, and special gifts. I can't imagine that any of you will have a personal quest as important as Buzz, but besides having faith in ourselves and helping others realize their potential, we should really know where our mission lies. If you don't know that and I suspect most don't, a little time should be spent every day to develop that concept. Think about who you are, where you have been, your current location, and where you want to be tomorrow. As long as you don't sell yourself short, the value of this simple daily process will change your life, bringing you unimagined personal prosperity.

My guarantee to you: If you actually follow through with this effort by spending a few minutes every day for a year and don't get positive results, contact Buzz or me at *Infinity and beyond*. We'll beam you up for a consultation. Life is filled with thinkers; great people who have worked with machines, money, ideas and other people for remarkable accomplishments. One of my favorites is Henry Ford. Without knowing us or Buzz, he once said, *If you believe you can or you believe you can't, you're right.* It's your life, you are responsible, and the choice is yours.

Listening with Shirley Romans

Shirley Romans is one of life's wonderful gifts. If we could place orders for the people in our lives, you would probably want the Shirley Romans' combo: friend, humorist, and tower of wisdom. As with a rock that spends lots of time being tumbled and tossed in a river's flow, Shirley is smooth and well rounded. She is the patina that artists use to express the richness of physical and spiritual beauty; there is a celestial glow which energizes her and those around her.

Shirley is on a roll, at age 90, she possesses a great attitude, splendid communication skills, happiness, love, patience, and a host of other splendid qualities.

A resident of Goodwin House West in Falls Church, Virginia, I met her to make a contribution. There was a fuzzy idea of benefiting her, but I couldn't visualize the specifics. After several visits to her assisted living center, our roles became clear. I was her listener, she was my inspiration.

There is much to be said about strangers who meet to explore, learn and grow from one another especially when there is diversity in age and gender. It can be a real crock pot of sentiments that if left to simmer and stew leaves a creation tasty and memorable.

Shirley is part of the national treasury that resides in assisted living centers and nursing homes across the USA. They are not buried treasure, no mysterious map is part of the intrigue, they await us with their warm stories of life's ups and downs with interesting twists and turns thrown in for good measure.

Educators tell us that 80 percent of what we learn is done through listening. If you had to choose between being an excellent listener or excellent speaker, which would you select?

Fortunately, we can choose to be both and that combined with positive attitudes is our contribution to the world. We need more great speakers, but far overshadowing that need is the urgency of finding more great listeners. People who patiently sit, listen, and grow – people who will jump into life's crock pot to simmer and stew. Shirley's words echo with me, *every person who has a listener in their lives is greatly benefitted.*

Cherokee Dreamer

On a recent flight from Washington, DC to Dallas-Fort Worth, I was flooded with good memories of Steve Martin. A Native American of the Cherokee Tribe, he loved animals, nature, and money.

Steve wasn't perfect, but he had a fun-loving spirit that made him friends everywhere. We met in Dallas years ago when both of us were Navy recruiters. Steve's beat was Dallas and I was assigned 125-miles east in Longview, Texas.

In spite of our differences, we became fast friends. He was quick, spontaneous, and a risk taker; I was quiet, fairly shy, and not much at sticking my neck out. During the next few years, I watched Steve operate. Besides being one of the top recruiters in Texas, he developed a family-owned business that included a parking garage in downtown Dallas, a herd of 150 Appaloosa horses, a trucking business, and several hundred acres of real estate at Cedar Creek Lake—a recreation area southeast of Dallas. He was also generous, whatever he possessed, including his phenomenally good personality, he was willing to share.

As our friendship grew and his need for cash flow increased, I became the proud owner of his pet Appaloosa, a beautifully colored stallion named Kelly Comanche. Regrettably, the risk-taking qualities Steve possessed and practiced kept his family seesawing between feast and famine. He always seemed to be just slightly overextended.

His goal was to become a millionaire and to that end he exercised courage to make risky decisions; and he maintained faith in his dream and abilities to achieve his goal. He gracefully bounced back from failures.

As I transferred from Texas in 1972, I returned Kelly Comanche free of charge and threw into the good deal of my Black and Tan hound, Peggy Sue. He was broke.

A year later, Steve was killed by accidental electrocution. He was 36 years old. For nearly 30 years, I've thought about him with an increasing appreciation for his personal qualities: courage, faith, and graceful acceptance of failure. He didn't make his goal, but at least he had one, a big one, and he worked diligently in that direction. His life, brief as it was, provides a good lesson.

Entrepreneurship is a wonderful art. In the context of business, it brings together an energizing set of ideas, people and money to achieve something of good purpose. We can all be entrepreneurs in our personal lives by bringing together dreams with energizing goals, plans, courage, and faith to compliment our education and environment. We can change the world with our ability to act out these dreams. There may not be a million dollar rainbow in our future, but just as in the case of Steve Martin, we will be remembered for what we gave not what we achieved for ourselves. Steve's legacy was inspiration and I now pass that to you for whatever purposes you wish to make of it.

A Blind Visionary

My earliest recollection is from 1946. It was summertime in Southeastern Michigan. I was nearly four years old and on an important mission with my grandfather, William Clay Aper. He and other farm hands had loaded a large wagon with loose hay that would later be used as winter fodder for livestock. Sitting high atop this load with my granddad, I helped him hold the reins to the two Belgian geldings pulling hard to move us forward.

The wagon was a turn of the century model with steel rimmed wooden wheels that caused the load to sway as the creaking wheels rolled over imperfections in the country lane.

Both of the Belgian geldings were named Dick, one blind and the other with vision. As a child and preteen I often watched them as they worked, played, and ate. Looking into their eyes I wondered what they felt, especially Blind Dick. He had been born without sight and shortly after being foaled, my grandfather aligned him with another young horse, Dick. The two had experienced so much together they were like one, as the sighted helped the blind.

Vision can take different forms. There are images that our eyes and brain process and there are the dreams and imaginary views of the future that we create mentally. Both are miracles.

My friend Jim Thune is a blind visionary. As with the horses, I have a strong memory of him, especially him passing me in the 1995 Cherry Blossom 10 Miler in Washington, DC. As a blind runner, Jim had a sighted guide and we spoke briefly as he powered on by at the 4-mile marker.

Jim was a wonderful friend, gardened, built his own patio, and was a terrific runner—one year he even did the Marine Corps Marathon. Jim's eyes didn't function, but he had vision and could eloquently describe what he felt. It was wonderful being with him;

we mentored one another much as Dick and Blind Dick worked together.

A few years ago, Jim moved from his home in Northern Virginia to Texas in pursuit of new directions.

These memories illustrate how well nature and people combine to create wholesome visions. People and animals share their strengths to the betterment of all. It doesn't happen automatically, it occurs because we make choices for their partnership; Jim and I chose to work together to the betterment of each other and those around us. We often call this mentoring and I supposed that's as good a tag as any. It is important to be mentored and to help others through a sharing of experiences. Being involved in mentoring is a conscious choice, not an automatic response. We actually extend ourselves to develop talents by seeking the right match to help us and to find those who we can help. Ideally, those on the path of personal growth have at least two mentoring relationships. One is primarily focused on benefiting you and the other deals with helping someone else. The nature of vision and mentoring may require a change in your style of personal management, but for those involved there will be handsome rewards. It's your life, you're responsible, and making the choice to create your best opportunities for success is solely your own.

Drowning in Data

TV, radio, recorded music, newspapers, books, magazines, videos, video games, Internet, office documents, telephone calls, mobile text messages, junk mail. Do you feel trapped or at least smothered with the amount of information flowing through your life?

A recent study from the University of California, Berkley, uses the term *drowning in data* to describe our plight. In an article entitled, *Information everywhere, but not the time to think,* Elizabeth Weise wrote in *USA Today* (Oct 19, '00) that if all the information *were ...divided up among every man, woman and child on the planet, it would require that each be given the equivalent of a library of 250 books.*

Finding space to learn in this sea of information is a breathtaking challenge. To free up quality time for learning, why not try your commute with a wonderful set of motivational tapes or the latest recorded bestselling book? This idea isn't new and it isn't for everyone.

A year ago, I unplugged the television, bought some books and have become reacquainted with the miracle of learning. Several weeks ago, a generous friend gave me *The Weekend Seminar, Skills for the 21ˢᵗ Century*. I've listened to the 12 cassette tapes once and am half-way through the second listening. As a result, I am well on my way to being transformed and three friends have asked to use the tapes when I am finished. In the *weekend seminar*, author and business philosopher Jim Rohn recommends skills for the 21ˢᵗ century, which by the way would have been wonderful skills for the 20ᵗʰ century.

Rohn has marvelous ideas and a pleasant manner in expressing ideas that inspire the imagination, more belief in ourselves and others, create a more positive lifestyle, improve communications, manage time with greater clarity, and set goals that have meaning.

Learning about ourselves and others contributes to our success in relationships, day-to-day prosperity on the job, how far we'll travel in life and the quality of the journey. Learning is about choices, we can allow ourselves to be smothered with information or selectively sort through it to find the nuggets of gold that will nurture our personal growth.

Ms. Weise's title, *Information everywhere, but not the time to think*, was right on target, but it doesn't have to be that way for people who make good choices.

Three Close Friends

In a recent article in *Sea Services Weekly*, Chaplain Herman G. Platt, described an interesting concept. Chaplain Platt wrote that he'd read somewhere that *....each of us needs at least three close friends whose faces light up when we enter the room.*

He went on to relate that the qualifications for this scenario were that you can't count family members, or friends who live more than 100-miles away, or those you see less than once a year. How do you stack up?

These thoughts give an open-ended theme that can be taken in many directions. We can think of those in our lives and how often we treat one another as stars who illuminate social settings; we could question the wisdom of having at least three close friends by asking, *who says and why?*

Or an argument could be made that more than three close friends are needed to develop grace and style, help socialize us, contribute to our emotional intelligence, promote our self-esteem and confidence, give us an outlet for disappointment and frustration, tell us when we're wrong and defend us when our behavior or judgment should have been better.

These friends are our buddies, mentors and confidants, celebrate our heroism, hold our hands in comfort and help fuel our flight to cloud 9. An extensive network of friends gives us our sense of community, teaches sharing and compassion, leads are humor workouts, and provides inspiration.

Friendships for me have been the irreplaceable kind that leaves indelible memories saved up for quiet moments of reflection. I am convinced that my progress through life has been charmed because, most generally, there has always been a cadre of caring friends nearby. In many ways, the year 2000 has been my best, in other ways it's been less that it could have been, either way you look at it friends make a huge difference.

They make the good times better and the bad times less burdensome. If having a companion or two on the roller coaster of life is an import value to you, the world is a cornucopia of humanity just waiting to be of service. All you have to do is be there with a spirit of optimism and human nature will take its course. Every person you meet has the potential to be a wonderful friend if you're willing to be a good friend in return.

Dr. W. Edwards Deming

It was seven years ago, December 20, 1993, that Dr. W. Edwards Deming passed away. At the time he was 93 years old and still conducting seminars in Total Quality Management until 10 days before his death.

Dr. Deming was one of those larger than life characters that we chance upon too seldomly; he was a heroic business philosopher who continues to have an incalculable impact on our lives. For starters, he was responsible for revitalizing Japanese industry following World War II and he was the man who ultimately sparked the third wave of America's industrial revolution.

That he influenced our quality consciousness on a large scale is an understatement. The business survival and prosperity by management and workers at many of our best known and most respected institutions owe their livelihood to Dr. Deming. Ford Motor Company, Motorola, Xerox, Westinghouse, Federal Express, Texas Instruments, and American Telephone and Telegraph are but a few of the organizations that were transformed by his ideas.

The cornerstone of his beliefs revolved around communications with management listening to the words of rank and file employees. He also believed workers should be empowered with responsibility to make decisions affecting their work centers. There were more simple concepts in Total Quality Management that involved having a trained and capable workforce and the use of statistical analysis to improve quality. But the big things were communications— listening and speaking up; and taking responsibility.

Much of corporate America failed to fully absorb Dr. Deming's concepts and that's unfortunate. He was an irascible change agent who went against the grain of conventionality. People being what they are, managers often felt threatened at the thought of giving up responsibility, others, including the rank and file employees, simply didn't have the skill or inclination to speak with confidence or listen with empathy. Has the world changed much in the past seven years?

As a no-nonsense teacher, Dr. Deming would probably have thought it frivolous, but just a few days before he died, *Washingtonian* magazine voted him one of the 25 smartest people in Washington, DC. In a city of smart people, that's quite a distinction. There's a lot that impressed me about Dr. Deming's philosophy, most prominent was that communications, the ability to articulate with conviction, the ability to listen with understanding and appreciation, were given prime emphasis in management-employee interface.

We intuitively know communications is vital to the human experience, but mostly we continue to relegate its importance to the back burner, a place that might or might not be visited in the future. Just as it costs business when communications are poor, each of us pays a dear price when the quality of our personal communications is less than it should be. Thanks to Dr. Deming's teachings we are more aware of the value in team work and promotion of harmony, both key to mankind's greatest achievements.

Helen Keller

Life is an amazing place, everyday at least one person brings something uplifting. It might be an unusually kind word or chance observation of a special deed, or something that causes us to blink in wonderment at the generosity of our fellow beings. We are all highly fortunate to be on this treadmill of inspiration.

But the days I really love bring an extraordinary experience, something that propels me higher than I normally cruise. You know what I mean, you see or learn something that is so profound and utterly good you can scarcely contain yourself. I call that level of excitement jumping out of your skin.

Over the past three weeks, I've had such an experience in reading the book, *Helen Keller, A Life*, by Dorothy Herrmann. As a late bloomer, I am probably one of the last to realize that Helen Keller was such a magnificent human being who enriched everyone by her example. She was a deaf-blind whiz kid brought to life by another extraordinary personality, Annie Sullivan, teacher and companion for nearly 50 years.

I can't tell you what it's like to be entombed in darkness and silence yet illuminate the world with your radiance. Because she lived it, Helen Keller is the only one who can describe that experience. In her life, she was an author, lecturer, actress, humanitarian, and activist for racial integration, peace, respect for human dignity, and caring and education for the disabled, especially the deaf-blind.

In a life of high achievement, one of her finest hours came as an honors graduate at Radcliffe College, the first deaf-blind person to graduate from college. She loved the world which returned that affection in all of the 34 countries she visited with her message of hope for the disabled.

Presidents, kings, the wealthy and everyday people were enriched by her presence. Some said that when meeting Helen they felt they were in the presence of a saint. There is a relatively small group of deaf-blind. In the world during the past 100 years, there are fewer than 50 deaf-blind people who developed the condition in very early childhood. That makes Helen unique.

She is also unique because of her eloquence in describing life and people that she couldn't see or hear, she could only feel them in her heart and express that through her writings and lectures. In her life (1880-1968), she became a monumental symbol of faith to millions of disadvantaged people. Her personal example of inner joy and optimism breaks a trail we should all be pursuing.

In the shadow of Helen Keller, we can more easily find the sureness of our own footing, especially if we're prone to discouragement and denial that we can be triumphant with most things in our life. *Helen Keller, A Life*, is available in bookstores and Amazon.com. It's there for you when you want to have an extraordinary experience, something life jumping out of your skin.

As a complement to the book rent the 1962 movie, *The Miracle Worker*, starring Anne Bancroft as Teacher and Patty Duke portraying Helen. Both Bancroft and Duke earned Oscars for their acting. A second movie, *The Miracle Worker*, was recently released by Disney; it also captures the frustration of an unhearing, unsighted but gifted child who wants to communicate. Through whatever media you choose, Helen Keller will remind you of what an amazing place life can be.

The Gift of Life

On a Sunday afternoon 20 years ago, four young men paddled two canoes along a gently flowing Potomac River. Two were 18, one 19, and another 20 years old. Near Glen Echo, Maryland, they saw signs that boats were not allowed further along the river because of a dam ahead.

The water was calm; it didn't look dangerous, the boys made a bad choice. They continued to paddle on enjoying a beautiful blue sky, lovely tree lined banks, and gently flowing water. Then they heard the rush of water and felt the boats surged forward, unable to escape the undertow the lead canoe cascaded over the dam, dropping four feet and capsizing. With difficulty the second canoe maneuvered to shore.

The dam was nicknamed the mix master because its concave construction is designed to create a cyclical motion to pulverize debris floating downstream. The two boys wore lifejackets but were caught in the water's turbulence. They were pulled beneath the surface, battered against the dam, surfaced and the process repeated again and again.

Once ashore, the other two young men took immediate action. While one went for help, the second jumped into the water to save his friends. He then found himself caught in the churning action.

The Glen Echo Rescue Squad quickly responded to the emergency, but it was too late for the three men. Family and friends were devastated. These were wholesome, smart and good kids. Every day we read about the tragic loss of life from accidents, war, starvation, and disease. It happens so often that we are often jaded and don't give another death second thoughts. That is unfortunate. More people need to recognize the precious nature of life without having to go through the trauma of having it threatened.

Last month, I had the opportunity to attend a retirement reception in Leonardtown, Maryland. My luncheon companion was Joan Mattingly, a retired nurse and cousin of the honoree, Shirley Mattingly. In our conversation, she mentioned how terribly abusive people were to themselves with overindulgence in alcohol, prescription and nonprescription drugs, and food. To make matters slightly worse we're not getting enough exercise. That wasn't the first time I'd heard such sentiments but coming from a health care professional that had spent her career treating overindulgence, I was more impressed.

When we don't follow appropriate prescriptions for physical and mental health we are disrespecting ourselves. That's what low self-esteem is about, giving ourselves less respect than we deserve. Be that as it may, it's important to recognize that this life is all we will ever have, it may be gone tomorrow. Each of us must work toward our happiness and fulfillment in life, no one else will do that for us, we are personally responsible. If we let ourselves become overweight or don't exercise our mental agility, we are disrespecting the gift of life. If we treat others poorly, if we don't extend ourselves to help others, we are disrespecting the gift of humanity. Everyone makes choices in how they will live; disrespecting the gift of life is not a good decision. In being our best starts with respect for ourselves and those around us. When we do that everything else naturally falls into place.

Brainpower

Last week I successfully completed another search for my ATM card. For the past several years that's been a quarterly experience. This time, I found it at the Resource Bank in Herndon, Virginia, just where I had taken my last cash withdrawal. For the uninitiated, if you take your cash and leave your card, the machine sucks it back in for safekeeping.

But I can do more than lose my ATM card. Car keys disappear at the rate of one set per month, and my glasses sprout wings and take flight weekly. I used to blame myself, but then switched to my brain as if we were really two separate entities.

Now I've matured to realize that I've grown a little absent-minded when it comes to remembering every small detail. And I must apologize to my brain which certainly has more important matters than focusing on the minutia of keeping me cruising down the road with cash in my pocket. We should all love our brains and respect the amazing power these on board computers possess.

One thing I enjoy most is the way the brain processes our five senses. Take the eyes for example. Almost constantly changing images, like movies, enter the retina, are transmitted to the brain, which determines shape, color and distance in nanoseconds. The brain does that while performing hundreds of other functions, all simultaneously.

Another of the things our brain does is learning incredibly fast from an assortment of stimulus. That starts at birth and each day for the first four years, our knowledge of the world doubles. Isn't that awesome?

If there is a downside to all this it's that we learn lessons in negativity just as quickly. Parents, teachers, and friends help us develop fear, feelings of inadequacy, and hopelessness. That makes our life as adults more difficult. Besides having to compete with others for our share of financial well-being, love and attention, we've got to overcome all the poor programming that our smart on board computer picked up along the way. With the potential for information overload is it any wonder that I lose a few things now and then? How about you? Ever feel a little overwhelmed by it all?

Fortunately, there are a few basics that can somewhat compensate for those early years of programming that displaced our self-confidence. One idea that works well is to hang with positive people which may require you to shed a few negative relationships. Liberating yourself from relationships that restrict your growth, learning and sense of well-being is vital.

Another thing, read good books, books that inspire you to improve yourself. Read biographies, read about the ideas that others have for self-improvement, learn what has benefited people in similar situations and apply it to your life. Lastly, knockoff negative self-talk, don't put yourself or anyone else down. We're all fairly brilliant, how could we be anything else with all that brainpower?

None of these ideas is guaranteed to spare you searching for lost cards, keys or glasses, but they will change your life for the better. You will be more satisfied and happy with a sense of well-being that will be a personal showcase. That I can guarantee!

When Opportunity Knocks

I saw her coming up the walk, a white envelop in each hand, then came the soft knock. This was indeed a special occasion as Shannon announced that she wanted to come in for a minute to deliver cards she had made.

One was a Father's Day card and the other a birthday card five months early. Inviting her in, I knew there was a problem as about every six weeks or so she and I repeat this cycle. Asking if she was bored, a long sigh preceded a softly murmured, *yeah!*

It isn't often that Shannon, age 6, reached out for my friendship. When it happens, I get mixed feelings. A part of me is complimented by the idea of being looked upon as a friend, and another part realizes the importance of friendship responsibilities.

I offered her a bowl of ice cream to which she responded, *Yeah, I guess so.* That was followed by a Disney movie, *Dinosaur;* lunch; another movie, *Charlies Angels;* popcorn; 8 or 9 games of Connect Four; a music video by *The Corrs;* dinner; and completion of a 100-piece puzzle with the Coca-Cola bear. In between, there was chit-chat about school, her family, rabbits, fish, her father's vegetable garden, soccer, travel to Ireland and she asked my opinion of people who lie.

Betsy McManus, Shannon's mother called every few hours to check on us. Seven hours later, I mentioned that it was time that we bid one another happy trails.

Shannon responded, *Well, I was sorta hoping that I could spend the night.* Unconsciously, one of my eyebrows raised and a faint smile appeared, but I stuck to my right to enjoy a small degree of privacy in what remained of a Saturday.

The moral of this story is that when people bestow the honor of friendship upon us we also become somewhat responsible. When duty calls, I think it's important to respond in the best fashion we can.

I have had strangers decide they needed my friendship and people I thought didn't like me demonstrate a need for fellowship. Stranger, foe, family member or acquaintance, we have a responsibility to nurture our fellow beings when the need arises. Most of the time, we don't think much about our kinship to humans, much of our life is spent in a vacuum, even demonstrating an everyman for himself mentality; we gossip, say hurtful things, and fail miserably in our human relations. We don't know our neighbors, won't make eye contact or smile or talk to strangers. When we perceive that there is an inequity on the highway, we make obscene gestures and can create enough pandemonium that people die in the aftermath. None of this is rational, it just doesn't fly. What does fly is extending yourself when you hear that soft knock.

The opportunity that Shannon presented, the honor and responsibility, literally came from a gentle knock on the door; you can also experience it through eye contact, a touch, or a sense of intuition. We all need one another, young and old, male and female, it makes no difference.

Shannon presented me a wonderful opportunity to be my best as a friend, these things happen to all of us every day. I don't always respond at my best, I need work but I believe we all do and it starts with just being aware that people have needs that we can fulfill. It doesn't usually take seven hours of friendship to help someone, often a smile, touch on the arm, or a few kind words are enough to make a huge difference.

After Shannon left, she returned 10-minutes later. In her hand was a helium balloon that said *Happy Father's Day*, it may as well have said, *Thanks for being my friend.*

Life Looks Like Fun

Last week I had the opportunity to work in 90-degree heat building a 6-foot privacy fence in a neighbor's backyard.

I had just started painting the finished product when sisters Erika and Phyllis Martin and Akua Adutwumwaah chanced along. Ranging in age from 10 to 12, they asked an important question, *Whatcha doin?* When a child asks that it could mean several things: 1) they already know the answer; 2) they want to be involved; or 3) like adults, they want to make conversation.

I explained the painting process to which I heard the chorus, *Can we help?* Relieved of paint, brush and roller, the girls gleefully went to work and I changed jobs to cleaning up the work site.

Fifteen minutes later, hot, sweaty and fading fast, I overheard someone say: *When you see people painting it always looks like so much fun.* Another girl added, *but it's really lots of work.*

These young ladies learned a good lesson that day. They will probably forget it, but there will be reminders all through their lives that much of what we see looks like fun, but is actually burdensome. It looks like fun to be rich, fly an airplane, go to college, be a doctor, learn a foreign language, play a musical instrument, or become a diva, but all of these fun-oriented worthy achievements require incredible discipline, perseverance, and sacrifice.

In short, before the fun begins we must work hard. Or we could find fun in work. That makes more sense, but requires that we carefully choose our endeavors. Making good choices is as simple as reading lots of books and meeting lots of smart people. Simple rules like closing our mouths, listening, reading, watching and striving to understand can lead anyone to a place called *life is fun, work is rejuvenating.*

We're lucky because we are surrounded with others just like us who provide positive examples, give us energizing ideas, pat us on the back when we do well, and lend a bit of constructive criticism now and then.

All the lessons we will ever need about choices and living a rewarding life have already been documented in the lives of our predecessors over the past 2,000 years. These basic ideas are delivered in new packages everyday as life changes and new interpretations of old ideas are developed. My suggestion is to read good books and hang with good people. You'll find that life not only looks like fun, it really is! However, as good as it can get, I am not guaranteeing that anyone will ever love painting a fence in 90-degree heat. Erika, Phyllis and Akua would probably agree.

A Reason, a Season, or a Lifetime

About 18 months ago, I received the following essay by Russell Dipasquale via the Internet. I've read it often to be reminded of the high value that our relationships have if we contribute patience, understanding and nurturing.

Everyone is connected to everyone else; if we manage our relationships well connections propel us forward in learning and appreciation for life's bounties. If we want to receive the best, we must give the best. The quality of our relationships determines the quality of our lives. This essay helps us understand the process.

"People come into your life for a REASON, a SEASON, or a LIFETIME.

"When you figure out which it is you know exactly what to do.

"When someone is in your life for a REASON, it is usually to meet a need you have expressed outwardly or inwardly. They have come to assist you through a difficulty, to provide you with guidance and support, to aid you physically, emotionally, or spiritually. They may seem like a Godsend, and they are.

"They are there for a reason, you need them to be. Then, without any wrongdoing on your part or at an inconvenient time, this person will say or do something to bring the relationship to an end. Sometimes they die. Sometimes they walk away. Sometimes they act up or out and force you to take a stand. What we must realize is that our need has been met, our desire fulfilled, their work is done. The prayer you sent up has been answered and it is now time to move on.

"When people come into your life for a SEASON, it is because your turn has come to share, grow, or learn. They may bring you an experience of peace or make you laugh. They may teach you something you have never done. They usually give you an unbelievable amount of joy. Believe it! It is real! But, only for a season!

"LIFETIME relationships teach you lifetime lessons; those things you must build upon in order to have a solid emotional foundation. Your job is to accept the lesson, love the person/ people (any way); and put what you have learned to use in all other relationships and areas of your life. It is true that love is blind – but friendship is clairvoyant."

Red, White and Blue

Monroe, Michigan is one of thousands of little towns in America that raise heroes, hard-working young people that rise to become tomorrow's courageous leaders. The ornate Victorian homes and towering maple and oak trees don't hint to origins of humble French missionaries and furriers who traded with the Chippewas, Sauk, and Ottawas.

Driving Main Street, particularly the residential neighborhoods you garner a sense of character that so many of our little American town's possess. This is a place of thoughtful people and good kids that represent crops of heroes starting small, but forced to grow with events they don't well understand.

David Nichols, his sisters Ashley and Erin, and Colin Hagen live there among the quiet residential streets. In the several days following the Trade Center and Pentagon attacks of 9/11, young David, 8, told his mother he wanted to go door-to-door collecting money for the terrorist victims. Lea Ann Nichols is a mother who positively affects her children. She suggested that they offer something of value when asking for a donation. The kids put their heads together deciding to braid key chains with red, white and blue beads and give candy decorated in red, white and blue ribbon.

On Sunday afternoon, September 16, they started down their street for a journey around the block. David carried the American flag; his sister Ashley, 6, brought the money jar with red, white and blue ribbons and "God" written on the side; Erin, 3, provided the tambourine beat which alternated with the drum she also toted along. Colin packed the give-aways. As they marched from door-to-door, the kids took turns being the spokesman. Speaking at her first home, Erin managed to blurt out, *Give me all your money!* She was rewarded with $10, eyebrows of her fellow crusaders went up as they looked at one another and then at Erin curiously.

Half a block further at her second shot in the lead role, she had learned better self-expression by explaining that they were collecting money ...*for kids who had lost their daddys.*

That night, after the kids had raised $220, David had never had more self-confidence or self-esteem. He had done something remarkable. As mom tucked him into bed, he asked, *Mommy, when I grow up do you think I should join the Army or Navy?*

This story touched me not only because Lea Ann is my niece and they were her children, but it was also the observation that David grew by exercising his goodness of spirit and in the process he positively influenced everyone around him. His admirable example suggests that we all learn from one another, everyone is our teacher, children help adults, the poor teach value to the rich, and the ill benefit the healthy.

There are no limits or boundaries to our learning when we embrace the miracles in human nature that can be taught and learned. Life is made so interesting that way because of point and counterpoint, the power of polar opposites and thinking out-of-the-box about intuition and the unlikely aspects of counterintuition that we encounter every day.

The Human Experience

The human experience has been in high gear during the past several months. Starting with 9/11, there have been dramatic changes that will fill thick history books with descriptions of transforming events and leadership.

The narratives will loom large in presenting dynamics that reframed past paradigms. Other occurrences will only be noted in our personal journals and family histories. We're privileged to be alive at this time to experience a shrinking world with people expanding their understanding, respect and decency toward one another.

Starting with an act of obscenity by a Saudi Arabian lunatic, we've seen American leadership shine with conviction to enforce justice while being judicious in restraint. We've received lessons in religion, international politics, lawlessness, fanaticism, geography, compassion, and human behavior. Our vocabulary has been expanded to fluency in pronouncing the names of foreign luminaries and out-of-the-way cities, towns and provinces.

There have been shocking revelations and mild surprises. Some of us became depressed, started overeating and stopped shopping, many lost their jobs and everyone felt more like they were on a rocket ship speeding through time with an uncertain destination. People have stayed home more, hugged their kids with greater passion while snuggling between spouses has been more vigorous.

Movie rentals and the sale of ice cream are both up; gasoline prices and airline travel are down. George Harrison died of cancer. As a result, we were treated to several days of refreshing Beatlemania to rediscover the wonder of four average teenagers from England who developed extraordinary talent as musicians, poets, and philosophers.

On the world's small stage, Jordan Riley was killed in an automobile accident in Atlanta. A young man in his freshman year at Tuskegee University, Jordan had been an 8-year volunteer at the National Race for the Cure, a breast cancer benefit, in honor of the women in his family.

Chrissie Carrigan, 15, took her own life. The sister of Trevia-Lynne Carrigan and her husband, Peter Colwell, Chrissie was a good, decent kid who attended Northwestern High School at Germantown, Maryland. Her classmates were devastated; no one knew the burden she carried.

Lois Addy died in Saluda, South Carolina. It was expected that Lois would be leaving us one of these days; she was 109 and had been the babysitter for Senator Strom Thurmond.

When personal and world events happen in rapid succession it is hard to maintain perspective in understanding what it all means and how it's connected. Every day we wake up to a new world where we apply our old world paradigms. We generally don't like change within ourselves or our environment, and it's difficult to accept the inevitability of life cycles.

Our discomfort with change makes life hard for us as change is the only constant, it's often not in our control but it's the only thing we can count on. How we meet new sets of circumstances is what determines our success at leading a happy, satisfying life.

Another factor at work is timelines. None of us know how long we will live. Some live a few days, others 15 years, and people like Lois Addy go 109 years. That's what makes life precious. It is also the reason we want to resist giving in to anger, anxiety, fear, or greed.

Our value to the world is derived from what we can give, not what we get. When we fail to give our best we are failing at rising to our highest personal value. When we learn to be joyful for each day of living and give our best to one another, we develop confidence in the future trusting that everything will work out. Giving our best to others is when we lend a voice to the speechless, strengthen the weak, and respect the dignity of those who find that quality in short supply. Giving our best is speaking up and taking action to protect children, the elderly, and those who are hungry and sick.

On our journey, we'll meet all kinds of people that are part of the human experience, each will make choices, and some of those decisions will affect us. In response we can choose anger, anxiety, fear, or greed; or the alternative, giving confidence, faith and trust. Which sounds best to you?

The Christmas Season

These are the best of times, it is the holiday season with twinkling lights brightening our neighborhoods, we're watching the joy of little kids validating our belief that they will grow to become big kids like us, and the sound of music from Tony Bennett, Destiny's Child and Charlotte Church touch us with emotion and romance of the season.

Love is in the air, love for one another and love for food; the more-the better, fattening is okay, it's the holiday season; we can relax enjoying our friends, families, co-workers, and neighbors. For a few days we are transformed in thought and deed, we're more prone to let that big innocent, kind-hearted kid in us out for all to see. Men play with trains like little boys, women who find kitchen environments unfriendly dread the chores ahead, others jump to the task with a little girl's exuberant leap of faith that everything will turn out all right.

It's the season to wear red scarves and display the good-natured smiles we were stingy with earlier in the year, hug busy children, and think about our religious heritage. There is a rush to help the homeless, the number of volunteers is overwhelming, and they are turned away with encouragement to return after Christmas when the spirit of giving has diminished. Most will not!

We'll think about the comfort of being in the human family and maybe consider our personal legacy to those around us. What trace of good will we leave about ourselves, how will we be remembered?

Since September 11, we've discovered that we really do like one another, everybody hurts at some time in their life and that we have the power to make things better.

This year, more than last, we'll be grateful to the postman, our auto mechanic and the cashier who befriended us at the supermarket. We'll think about the teachers who give beyond the norm to help our kids and the ministers, priests, and rabbis who struggle to convey comfort and understanding during trying times.

The challenge we all face is packing up our generosity of spirit, our thoughtfulness of the holiday season and hiking away with it into the future. I don't think it is overactive Imagineering to believe we would all have happier, more satisfying lives with the trademark spirit of giving that we experience during this time. Can you imagine walking out on to life's stage every day with the purpose of making the world better through your charismatic smile, your playfulness, your willingness to give? Is that what you'd like for your future?

The simplicity of lights, kids, music and food can lead us to a season for change, a season for new beginnings. It is our individual responsibility, the world is ours to enjoy while promoting betterment in ourselves and those around us. That's the human experience!

The After-Christmas Spirit

This year's birthday party for Jesus was a cornucopia of prayer, rejoicing, sorrow, stretching, and living the life of a couch potato. There were those struggling in poverty, international leaders and small town heroes performing acts of faith, and a genuine striving to understand it all, or at least that slice of life that is our experience.

In the past few days there have been memorable family reunions, gifts exchanged, and people sadly missed. We've been with personalities who baffled us with delight and we learned about people who astonished us with their behavior.

Dimwit of the Week, Richard Reid of kaboom shoe fame, gave us new energy to wonder about other people on the planet while the crew and passengers of the airliner Richard tried to destroy joined a growing club of personalities who were at their best when it counted most.

Between tragedy, war, accidents and the aging process there were many loved ones missing at this year's family celebrations.

Her family and a host of friends missed Chrissie Carrigan. Several months ago, 15-year old Chrissie saved the life of a classmate by snitching when her friend said she was contemplating suicide. When learning that Chrissie compromised a trust, the friend was initially angry but after several weeks of emergency counseling, she embraced Chrissie with gratitude for her life. Her family believes that Chrissie gave so much to others there wasn't anything remaining for herself.

This year, about 30,000 people took their own lives, a disproportionate number were adolescents and the elderly.

During the holidays I visited my grandnephew and grandnieces in the Nichols family at Monroe, Michigan. David is 8; Ashley, 6 and Erin, 3. The three kids had waved the red, white and blue while canvassing their neighborhood in September to raise $220 for victims of the 9/11 terrorist attacks. Checking in with the small fry, I learned that Ashley's hero is Harry Potter and David's hero is President George W. Bush, two good choices.

On December 20, President Bush took time to visit Martha's Table in Washington to deliver a speech short on policy, but long on heart. He thanked volunteers who help the homeless and others less fortunate and used Martha's to illustrate the importance of love and compassion to care for those less fortunate. Empirical data indicates that homelessness is growing rapidly; statistics say there was a 13 percent increase across the USA this year while the Washington homeless population increased 32 percent.

In the category of holiday love and compassion, a few days ago, I learned that Curt and Renee Darrow of Monroe, Michigan, refused to exchange holiday gifts. In lieu of bombarding each other with material comforts they can well afford, Curt and Renee adopt a needy family not just this year, but every year.

During the holidays, one family in Northern Virginia sadly learned that their 55-year old husband, father, brother, and friend had been diagnosed with leukemia just a few months before his planned retirement. When you have the opportunity to donate to medical research, take it. Research into causes and treatments for our most stubborn diseases like leukemia is central to a more secure future for our kids. If you want to say a prayer for Don, the family would be very grateful.

On the travel front, some people in the south were tempted to bring their tans north for the Christmas holiday, some in the Midwest went south for sea cruises, Disney World or to visit family.

If our southern brethren mistakenly went to Buffalo, New York, they may not return home until spring. With 73-inches (6-feet) of fluffy, white stuff over a 5-day period, I imagine they are now thinking about the possibilities of escaping by dog sled. There were lines at airports, long ones, shoes were checked, bag searched, smiles exchanged and a little carping took place. It's the sniffles and sneezing season; some have the flu or are recently recovered. I don't feel too healthy myself.

During the past week, two people standout. Mattie Stepanek is 11-years old and an award winning poet. Two of his most popular works are *Heartsong* and *Journey Through Heartsong*. Known as a poet and peacemaker, his hero is President Jimmy Carter, an admiration that President Carter returns. Mattie suffers from a rare form of muscular dystrophy which has taken the lives of two brothers and a sister. To learn more about this remarkable child visit www.vspbooks.com.

Dr. Sima Samar, Vice Chair for Women's Affairs in the new Afghan government is an articulate, no-nonsense and compassionate spokeswoman for her sister's rights in Afghanistan. Dr. Samar is also part of the miracle that is playing out in the New World of respect for human dignity. In America, Laura Bush, is her ally.

With over 13 million women who have suffered horribly under the Taliban, Dr. Samar leads the movement for full equality, a concept that is supported by over 90 percent of the male population.

As we think about a resolution for the New Year in an increasingly complicated world of human relations, the one statement we can make that will always be right, *Resolve to treat everyone you meet with kindness, whether they deserve it or not.*

New Year's Extraordinary People

New Year's found friends skiing in the west, others sunning themselves in Florida, men asked their favorite friends to New Year's Eve dinners, women did the same; some went to see *Harry Potter* and *Lord of the Rings*; kids struggled to stay awake with families up late to toast in the New Year; there were fire crackers, fireworks, and one or two shotgun blasts.

Sailors, Soldiers, Marines, and Airmen had a breather, but wondered about tomorrow; homeless dads, moms and kids shivering throughout the East and Midwest also wondered about tomorrow. Pete and Trevia Colwell cradled the handmade holiday gifts from their sister Chrissie Carrigan, now among the angels. There was the Rose Parade, football, and overindulgence.

Our European cousins can't talk enough about their new currency, which has proved popular with all including the world's criminal element. Crooks proved again that they know how to cleverly break the rules by stealing the new Euros before the official start date. And I wouldn't be surprised if at least several hundred terrorists around the world were not wondering about changing their career field.

Lisa Wollenhorst of Herndon, Virginia, is now resting her body, but working her head in mental preparation for the Bermuda

Marathon, January 20. Lisa has raised thousands of dollars for the Leukemia and Lymphoma Society to be a part of this hilly, 26.2 mile event.

New York's former mayor, Rudy Giuliani has been selected as *Time* magazine's Man of the Year, a well-deserved honor for his remarkable leadership during an extraordinary time in America. Mostly unpopular during the majority of his administration as New York City's mayor, he survived prostate cancer in 2000 developing a grace for humanity that he had not shown in earlier public life. A year later, he was called to inspire those working on survival of a different sort, the loss of loved ones. His authenticity, compassion and eloquence touched everyone—widows, widowers, children, world leaders, and those of us standing on the sidelines watching and wondering what it's all about.

Survivors bring us strength when we falter; they inspire, and carry the torch when necessary. Three-time breast cancer survivor Judy Pickett of Cameron Park, California will literally be carrying a torch, the Olympic one, on January 20 through the streets of Sacramento. At age 40, she is a national spokeswoman for faith, hope and optimism. Judy is a young woman not much different from Mayor Guiliani or anyone else who overflows with love for mankind.

Another three time breast cancer survivor, Di Keith Jones of Richmond, is planning her comments for January 23, when she'll be speaking to a gathering of volunteers for this year's Richmond Race for the Cure. At 48, Di is another activist who inspires with her heart and visionary focus on what's right and good about each of us. Inspiring leadership is a trademark of many survivors.

On December 20, 2001, Ernestine Ashley, a 16-year survivor, was honored as the 2001 Co-Volunteer of the Year, National Race for the Cure. Ernestine, who works for the Naval Space and Warfare Command, has led large volunteer teams from her agency, church, and neighborhood to support research and education programs of The Susan G. Komen Breast Cancer Foundation. She leads with an enthusiastic smile and genuine warmth; she's gorgeous and irresistible in personality, not much different from many other survivors.

Ada Palmer, now 17 years into a double survivorship, was the National Race for the Cure's 1999 Volunteer of the Year for her commitment to activate, initiate and captivate followers who were inspired by her enthusiasm to make the world better one day at a time.

Susan Sonley, a 7-year survivor, stands out in a group of extraordinary people. That's what makes her extra-extraordinary, a woman made for new words. Susan raised $60,000 in the past two years to benefit breast cancer programs. She's a driver like Vicky Martin Adamson of EDS in Herndon; Patti Brownstein in Great Falls; Rana Kahl, Manassas; Kim Henry, Silver Spring; and Connie Bash, Alexandria. All these volunteer fundraisers move mountains as though they were pebbles.

They have charisma just like Mayor Giuliani. If you're lucky enough to know a survivor, you have an excellent role model in life: Some of these sheroes I am fortunate to know are Grace Caliveer, Chris Colley, Amy Cruz, Roberta Culp, Fran Dockter, Margie Fehrenbach, Nancy Fosbrook, Kelly Gallagher, Maria Grenier, Rosa Harris, Vivian Hines, Eileen Kessler, Becky Kuhn, Lola Lawson, Judy Macon, Diane Mandell, Cheryl Mihal, Kathy Mills, Carmilla Mitchell, Mary Norwood, Jane Parham, Susan Shindeman, Marlene Sprigg, Beth Swanson, Fran Staiman, Gwen Talbot, Chris Thaler, Donna Weston, and Kim Wright.

They aren't famous like survivors Supreme Court Judge Sandra Day O'Connor, former first lady Betty Ford, Singer Diahann Carroll, or the nation's foremost breast cancer activist Nancy Brinker, but they all bring the same sense of calm and delight for the world around them.

Survivorship comes in big and small packages; everyone is a survivor of something. Frankly, I had a tough time with kindergarten because of a painful shyness, but that didn't threaten my life, it just scared the hell out of me. Surviving is not an American phenomenon and life threatening diseases don't have a monopoly on the process. Imprisonment and torture carries its burden. Afghan shero Soraya Parlika led an underground movement with 4,000 members to promote hope for women's rights. She spent 18 months in jail while captors coaxed her to snitch on those in her movement.

New Years is a resting place. We stop, think and move in new directions, some of you will choose a straight narrow course like railroad tracks, while others will select circular paths. But if you decide to develop the wings required for soaring, study a survivor who has had to cope with horrible threats to their well-being and see how they do it. Helping each other with a good example is one of the best parts of our human experience, taking their example as our own persona is the equation's other half.

Personal Prosperity

I'm terrified that I won't get as much compensation as everyone else, she said. That snippet was taken from an interview on public radio to describe the plight of a New York woman at accepting a government payment being offered to victim families of 9/11. The problem is that she had already accepted a large life insurance settlement that will decrease the government's formula for her and her 19-month old daughter.

In Argentina, citizens are rioting in the streets to protest not having full access to their savings accounts in a national financial crisis.

As they start life anew, Afghan government officials are expressing concern for their soldiers and civil servants who have not been paid in six months.

We continue to hear that in Washington and other large cities the need for food and shelter for the homeless is growing quickly. Fifteen years ago, in my first class of Economics 101, the professor made an interesting statement, *the great economic challenge is how to satisfy unlimited wants and needs with limited resources.* He never told us how to do it and I have not yet figured it out. Neither has anyone else! I also spent several years studying accounting and loved the challenge of balancing credits and debits. As it turns out, balancing columns of figures doesn't count as much as a high moral code.

Arthur Andersen auditors and Enron officials are shaking their heads and using finger pointing as gestures emphasizing, *No way, don't look at me, it wasn't my fault.* That's no satisfaction for the thousands of people who lost their jobs and pension funds, and investors who lost tens of billions of dollars in the Enron scandal.

In addition to the money, the world lost more faith in the integrity of people in high places. Before they start school, kids learn to point fingers and shake their heads no. As we grow, we get better at it but not much more convincing. Those who go into politics and big business continue the practice as part of their occupation, but most shouldn't be taken too seriously one way or the other. It's the bottom line that counts.

In spite of revolutionary world events, our human spirit hasn't changed much in the past four months, but we have captured glimpses of what we could be as patriots, spiritual devotees, and those who care deeply for the less fortunate. Integrity is another matter.

Following 9/11, people waved the red, white and blue; high-tailed it to religious services; and donated vast sums to the plight of terrorism victims and their families. The rhetoric notwithstanding, enlistments to support defense of America are not up; voluntarism and dollar contributions to help those less fortunate aren't up significantly; and after a spike in church attendance months ago, those visiting a house of worship is back to normal levels. Some social scientists believe Americans are on the brink of converting new cultural values to concrete actions that will change the world. That may happen, but it's up to us, one at a time to make that decision and take a new direction.

My view is the more we can give, the greater our personal prosperity. Waiting to have someone ask for help is not enough, we must proactively reach into our communities, look for nonprofit groups that help kids, provide creative activism for better health care, and seek ways to benefit the homeless and elderly. For those who aren't group oriented, find one person to strengthen through a sharing of your personal and financial resources. Lead where possible, practice inspiring yourself toward higher achievement, the result is that you'll inspire others in ways you can't imagine.

January 15 was Dr. Martin Luther King's birthday. Today, we celebrate his life with a holiday. If you are different, you can thank Dr. King for being able to walk with your head up without apology. Early in his life, he made the decision to connect with people were who angry, disappointed, frustrated, and poor. By following a path of nonviolent protest, he took a direction of leadership that guided Americans from the shadow of exclusiveness to lightness in recognizing human dignity. Now, if you're crippled, gay, uneducated, homeless, elderly, Black, brown, or yellow with pink hair, it makes no difference, you're better respected as a part of the human family.

None of us are perfect and neither is our society; however, because of Dr. King we are aware that respect for the diversity of human value is part of our American fabric. The concept of respect is taught in every public school and in religious institutions in our country. Dr. King was a bridge connecting our national leadership with everyone's conscience and the poorest among us; we were all enriched by the process.

Networking

On December 23, 2002, I was standing at the end of a line of people boarding a Delta flight from Cincinnati to Detroit. As I looked behind me, there was one person. We made eye contact, she smiled, I spoke. As luck would have it we were also seat mates. And that's how I met Floridian Shana Sikarskie and learned about the book, *Battlefield of the Mind*.

During the 60-minute flight we talked about many things, skipping enthusiastically from subject to subject until we hit upon emotional intelligence. That's when Shana pulled *Battlefield of the Mind* from her briefcase. She recommended the book; I've just finished it, found it enjoyable, and I think you will like it, too.

The genre is different from most books I've read; it combines biblical verse with the logic of modern day optimism. The integration of old with new provides the opportunity to explore how human values evolved through the lives of those who lived thousands of years ago.

Author Joyce Meyer is convinced that our goodness as well as dark lifestyles start in the mind, which converts thoughts to words and then to actions. Stated another way, negative thoughts ultimately manifest themselves in words and deeds that represent anger, fear, and self-doubt.

This negative-positive battlefield of our minds ultimately defines who we are, where we go, and who we hang with. Obviously, the polar opposite of negativity is faith, hope, love, optimism, and trust. Joyce believes we are in a constant struggle to stay positive. That's true, not much new there; however she packages her premise in fresh, new illustrations from her experiences as an evangelist. *Battlefield of the Mind*, educational and interesting, is a good book I recommend for those seeking self-improvement.

Several weeks ago, Terry Shen, a Washington, DC, friend with Toastmasters International spoke persuasively on the importance of networking through positive personal connections for win-win situations. Last summer, during another Toastmasters session, Pat West, gave a series of inspiring presentations that exposed her passion for network liaisons.

For my part, I'd say networking starts at birth and should progress well to the end of our days. The problem is that after childhood so many people stop connecting with strangers—eye contact with those we don't know is limited and smiles rarer yet. My connection with Shana Sikarskie is an illuminating example of real-life networking.

This time, two strangers meeting eye-to-eye shared a smile in a distant airport. In four weeks, she has offered advice to my niece, Lynn Freshour, on the best routes into pharmaceutical sales; given me good criticism on my new story, *The Kiss*; and I have sent her suggestions on having a chocolate fondue party. Shanna is charismatic, there's no doubt about it, but we don't need charisma to connect, only a sincere desire to listen, be heard, grow and learn. As Terry and Pat would agree, when we connect for the good of another, great things can happen; however, just as in the quality of our day-to-day communications, if we don't make the effort to do well, we may not be chancing upon the winning relationships that life provides.

The Lunatic Fringe

The BBC reports that Argentina has the highest per capita ratio of psycho-therapists in the world. That's a good thing given their national fiscal crisis that is preventing citizens' full access to their savings accounts. We don't need an upper level psychology-math course to know the equation of people minus money leads to depression. Complicating the problem, people don't have the money to pay for therapies so many of the Argentine shrinks are moonlighting as taxi drivers where they can deliver free advice along with the cab ride.

In Australia, Afghan refugees are also depressed. They are in austere camp settings and are waiting unusually long periods to learn if they will be accepted for immigration. There are hunger strikes, body mutilations, and mass suicide pacts. Those who look for things to complain about are also depressed or maybe they're happy, I can't tell.

Some people are focused on al-Qaeda and Taliban prisoners in Cuba saying that their open air, mesh wire cells resemble cages. They may well have never been better fed or cared for medically but that doesn't count, nor do the Korans we've provided or our Navy Muslim Chaplain who is administering to their religious needs. As much grief and heartache as they have caused, respecting human value hasn't stopped America from providing humane treatment for fanatics on the lunatic fringe; however, I can't imagine that life will get better nor should it for people who live to die in assassination of mass populations.

Truth

Several weeks ago, I wrote a piece about Argentina having the highest per capita ratio of psychiatrists in the world. I thought this was probably a good circumstance because of the economic slumber that is now driving the population there nutty with anxiety.

Well, it seems the polar opposite of Argentina may be Slovenia, a country of 2 million people, where a man was refused psychiatric help on January 31. When he was denied treatment at the hospital at Izola, Aleksandar Oven became angry, ran out of the hospital and returned minutes later in his car, which he drove through the glass doors and down a 30-yard corridor to reception. Asked why he did it, Oven told the truth, *I don't know – that's why I came here.*

Truth is a pervasive constant in our lives, so much so that we often take it for granted. Truth defines our humanity, our social structures, and the quality of our arts, economy, government, politics, spirituality, and sometimes our odd behavior. Even our relationships and inner sense of well being spin best on a basis of honesty.

Our great journalists are the backbone in a global network of communications that reaches even the homeless. Journalists are everywhere observing, reflecting, developing perspectives, and seeking truth. They're even there where people use the drive-thru for their psychiatric appointments.

We are now exposed to more information in one day than our grandparents received in a lifetime. It comes from the Internet, newspapers, magazines, television, and radio and it's mostly journalism. Sadly, journalistic truth took several steps backward in the past week. The Zimbabwe president, Robert Mugabe, is planning a cover-up.

The legislative branch there has reluctantly passed a new law to limit foreign journalist's access and reporting on future events in the country. The initiative is one in a series that President Mugabe is taking to cover-up a corrupt election he's planning in March. The 11-million people there are sick and tired of being morally bankrupt and want to elect the opposition. President Mugabe is desperate enough to make truth a casualty to his personal agenda.

Israel is limiting access of Palestinian journalists to events in the Gaza Strip, West Bank and Israel. I suspect this has much more to do with censorship than security.

In Pakistan, terrorist are making truth political in their kidnapping and threats to take the life of Danny Pearl, a model of journalistic integrity working for *The Wall Street Journal.* Besides observing and trying to sort through complex human issues for accuracy, many journalists have to be adventurers who take chances while soldiering in risky places. They are a brave army of writers, cameramen and women, and technicians. Along with the humanitarian missionaries of the International Red Cross, journalists and truth should never be taken hostage.

Truth may have taken a few steps backward this week, but Sherron Watkins is a growing monument to business integrity. Last year, Ms. Watkins, Vice President for Corporate Development at ENRON, raised the red flag to her superiors and counterparts at Arthur Andersen on accounting practices that didn't make sense. Last week, www.time.com selected Sherron as their Person of the Week.

I was recently in Florida consulting in my work with the Naval Criminal Investigative Service. President Bush was also in Florida promoting positive values in his encouragement for voluntarism. Every book on successful lifestyles that I've read in the past several years lists generosity of spirit, a giving to others, as the primary means to a happy, satisfying life. In my view, that is truth.

If you are not now formally aligned with a nonprofit organization, a neighborhood committee, or other community service organization, you're selling yourself short. And, of course, the world is needs the wonderful talent you have to offer. Giving money is okay, but donating talent is the ultimate fulfillment.

Several people I know are part of an extensive network involved in personal integrity. Di Keith Jones of Richmond is a 3-time breast cancer survivor who is among a group of distinguished survivors aligned for a Sunrise Award being presented by the American Cancer Society at an awards luncheon in Falls Church, Virginia, February 23, 2002.

Di possesses the seeds of greatness in her extreme enthusiasm to give faith, hope and optimism to other breast cancer survivors. In that process she inspires everyone around her.

Another truth sayer is Michelle James of McLean, Virginia, who will be speaking at this month's Women in Technology luncheon in Washington. Her topic is mentoring, one that she knows well. Not only did she create a cadre of personal mentors for herself over the years, but also gave a ton of encouragement to others.

Michelle and Di know the value of truth, good communications and positive attitudes. We're lucky to have them in our world.

Evil Spirits

Chinese everywhere are now celebrating the New Year of the Horse; it's their 4,700[th] year, a time for remembering Buddha, wearing red clothes and receiving money in red envelopes.

Red symbolizes fire, which according to legend can drive away bad luck. The Chinese in the People's Republic of China will be thinking about how they can rid themselves of evil spirits as millions of people are without work. Working, loving, and raising families in peace and security is a universal value that we all share regardless of skin color, religion, or geographic location.

In America, we also have our evil spirits that have contributed to over seven million people on the unemployment rolls. Some of the downturn is global economic adjustment, introduction of technologies that leave processes and jobs obsolete, changes in consumer demand, and errors in judgment. Like every country in the world we also have people who screw up because they're greedy and that impacts everyone economically.

On the side of selfishness, we have Enron's Kenneth Lay and Jeffrey Skilling. More recent estimates of his stock and real estate holdings indicate that Mr. Lay may be down to his last $43 million. Linda Lay, his wife, was recently on national television in hysterics because they are in financial ruin.

Last week, Mr. Skilling went before the American people in Congressional testimony to say he is emotionally devastated and innocent of wrongdoing. He spoke with conviction and sincerity in the pretense that as one of the most brilliant CEOs in America he just didn't know what was going on at Enron. Texas business philosopher, Dr. Ken Blanchard may have been thinking of people like Skilling and Lay when he wrote, *There is no right way to do a wrong thing.*

When confronting the hurt that dishonest businesspeople bring, it's good to remember Andrew Carnegie who once said, *He who dies rich, dies disgraced.* History tells us that Mr. Carnegie gave away his fortune of over $300 million to build 3,000 libraries and endow various cultural and philanthropic foundations to benefit the arts and world peace.

More recently, we can draw upon the inspiration of Aaron Feuerstein, owner of Malden Mills. In 1995, he saved the employment base of Lawrence, Massachusetts, by almost going broke keeping three thousand unemployed workers on the payroll and rebuilding his factories that were destroyed by a pre-Christmas fire.

His act of profound decency made him a national business hero. By putting his workers and their community ahead of his own financial self-interest, he demonstrated the highest level of business integrity and leadership.

It's also good to remember Boston businessman Tom White who is now down to his last 8 million dollars. During the past 50 years, he has given away $50 million to about 130 different charities. He particularly likes organizations that benefit the needy over institutions like museums and universities. Besides the money, Mr. White, 81, is personally involved in every charity he favors.

All of us have the capacity to be angels or devils, but we stay mostly in between the two extremes. Blind ambition and greed causes many people to demonstrate petty behavior. That doesn't make them worse than us, but when they are financially enriched on the backs of little people and are as unrepentant as Messrs. Lay and Skilling appear to be it makes us understandably angry.

University of Life

Courses started today at the University of Life, an interesting campus with stimulating opportunities for learning. The University starts new classes with new people every day, teachers there don't necessarily possess old fashioned degrees, those empowered by this institute of higher learning are children, neighbors, co-workers, spouses, the elderly—all are people that we've met or read about, they are either our friends or people we'd probably like to have as a friend.

By sharing their gifts and talents they are giving us worthy examples of generosity; in reading their books, we learn why change toward improvement is a lifelong path; in listening to their words we are compelled to rethink our paradigms.

The University extends its classrooms to our homes, offices and the streets, it's on the factory floor, hospital rooms, and in daycare, everywhere people congregate, a University mentor usually surfaces to present small pieces of life's educational puzzle. These relationships are complex as it happens that coaches and students swap positions, some days teachers teach, other days teachers reverse roles with students so that they can continue to learn and grow.

Although these life leaders are presenting lessons in faith, hope and optimism, not everyone is learning. Some of those exposed to this educational process should be developing self-confidence and self-esteem, but they aren't learning, they're goofing off in class. They have an attitude that says, *none of this applies to me, I am who I am, always have been, always will be.*

The University officials are troubled by the campus environment where some students are angry, arrogant, frightened, and insecure. They know they must work harder. The negative students aren't survivor material and they might slow the learning of the optimistic thinkers. However, the positive thinkers aren't hanging around with those who live in shadows.

What we've noticed about the honor students is that they are growing with a lightness that thrives on the warmth of human sunshine. They congregate together as people of enlightenment and influence. This core group is connecting the dots with a realization that happiness and satisfaction depends on the quality of interpersonal communications and the resulting relationships. If you don't feel like you're matriculated in one of the courses at University of Life, start today, pick up an inspiring book, listen to a friend, watch a child, or talk to a survivor.

Why Can't Everybody be Nice to Each Other?

Two years ago, Robbie Bolog, 12, of Milan, Michigan asked his grandmother, Marcia Bolog, *why can't everybody just be nice to each other?* Marcia didn't tell me what was said in response to this classic question, but Robbie is not alone in his curiosity and bewilderment at our behavior.

With over 6 billion people on earth and each of us possessing our own unique set of behavioral patterns, one simplistic answer to world disharmony is elusive; however, as members of the human family we do share common strengths and weaknesses. In my view, we can't be nicer because of arrogance, anger, envy, fear and selfishness that undermine our self-confidence and self-esteem.

We don't have all the respect we should for ourselves making it difficult to fully respect others. Top that off with an inability to forgive and forget past injustices and you've concocted a negative brew that will leave a hangover at times when we want to feel good about our relationships.

Author and psychologist John Gray believes that we carry an inner sewer filled with goop from our past. Negative experiences that we can't forgive may be temporarily forgotten as they slide into the sewer of our subconscious but these resentments reappear at the most awkward times in our future.

To give you an illustration, two weeks ago, I was en route home from work at the Washington Navy Yard. Traffic was light, but street construction slowed the progress of cars traveling east and west on "M" Street. At my first traffic light a man drove his van into the intersection and stopped because traffic was not moving. When the light changed, I signaled for him to back up so I could pass. Although no one was behind him, he shook his head and shrugged. In lieu of following my first impulse of pounding the fecal matter out of him, my jaws tightened, eyes narrowed, and I glared.

Giving me as good as I gave the other driver and I waited 20 seconds, traffic then moved allowing him to enter the flow of traffic. As he drove past me, I got the middle finger salute. Okay, I deserved the recognition for arrogantly believing that the 20 seconds I lost were more valuable than the time he gained by blocking traffic. Twenty seconds is not a lot to get upset about. Gray's sewer had backed up on me and I made another promise to better fight these impulses in the future.

One last complication, when we don't have the personal confidence to believe in ourselves, empathy suffers. We just don't understand and aren't open to understanding how other people feel. If we truly understood how cruel we are to one another, it wouldn't happen, and there wouldn't be little boys asking, *why can't everybody just be nice to each other?*

The good news: we can change, we can improve, and we can be the people we want to be.

I recently spent six days on business at Meridian, Mississippi. Meridian is the old south; population is 47,000, dog's legally run loose, no commuter traffic, and people smile and talk to strangers. This is in contrast to the new south which is characterized by people congestion, restrictions, overbuilding, and a tragic loss of nature.

The old and the new south do have similarities. In daily jogs past the Oak Grove Baptist Church in Meridian, I noticed that the minister had sent a message to passersby. The marquee said: *Wanted: ordinary people for extraordinary work.* Interestingly, my minister at the Trinity Presbyterian Church in the new south of Herndon, Virginia, presented a comparable message in his sermon a month earlier. Of course, we are much more than ordinary or extraordinary, we are brilliant; each of us is capable of making the most astounding contributions to the world. The problem is that we don't acknowledge that part of us or work in those positive directions where we have immense potential, particularly at *just being nice to each other.*

While in Meridian, I met Navy Lt. Tammy Mediate, a helicopter pilot at the local Naval Air Station. Weeks earlier she had appeared on ABC's morning talk show, *Live with Regis and Kelly* as part of a feature, *Makeovers for People in Uniform*. Unknown to Tammy, her mother, in Pennsylvania, had sent a picture and written an essay explaining why her daughter should be selected to be part of the show. From hundreds of submissions, she was one of five selected to appear on the show.

Robbie Bolog would be glad to know that Tammy said, *Regis is such a nice man...kind to everyone in helping them feel at ease.*

Joy Bright Hancock

In my dining room there are two pictures hanging on the wall. One is from 1919 and it shows young Joy Bright Hancock (1899-1984) at the start of adulthood. She's in a Navy Yeomanette uniform and was probably one of the most handsome women of her generation.

The second picture shows Joy at age 80, shining eyes, generous smile, and still beautiful. Following her World War I service, Joy had both a tragic and exciting life. Sadly, she was widowed twice as a young woman as two husbands were killed in naval aviation accidents, and her third husband in later life died of cancer.

Offsetting the sadness of her losses, she adventured, wrote, and painted as she traveled the world. One of her most inspiring journeys took place in 1925 on a 200-mile trek with an elephant and native guide to the ancient ruins of Angkor Wat in Cambodia. She was 27, small of stature, big in determination. On arrival at the ruins, she remained two months living in a tent to explore, sketch and take notes on her observations.

Joy traveled to Europe and the Far East on dollar liners, ships that took passengers for a dollar per day and the option to come aboard or disembark at any port of call.

In 1942, she patriotically returned to naval service. Underweight, overage and without a college degree, she applied for and was granted three waivers to earn a commission. Within 10 years, she had reached the rank of Captain and was the senior woman in the Navy.

March is Women's History Month, a good time to remember this unforgettable character.

I sought Joy out in 1982; she was 84 and residing at Vinson Hall, an assisted living center at McLean, Virginia. My intent was to enlist her to give a brief speech celebrating the 40th anniversary of women's permanent service to the Navy.

If ever there was the right candidate, Joy's credentials suggested that she was perfect for the job. She was a World War I veteran, widow to three naval aviators, a private pilot, author, artist, and Navy leader. From 1942 to 1953, she had served a second stint with the Navy eventually retiring as a Captain responsible for all women in the Navy.

Joy was a tiny, frail woman, still formal in her military protocol. The walls of her apartment were filled with oils of beautiful Impressionist seascapes she had done while living with her third husband in France.

When asked to be part of our speaking program, she was enthusiastic, but seemed so frail, I had reservations. At the time I was the public affairs officer at the Naval Security Station in Washington, DC, and at the center of planning the 40th anniversary program.

There would be a large audience, entertainment, and two main speakers. After insisting that I send her a formal invitation from my commanding officer, she accepted.

The day arrived and a Navy car picked Joy up at her home. The program's first speaker didn't bring the inspiration I had envisioned to make the program memorable, but I still had Joy.

Upon being introduced, the audience gave her a warm welcome of applause as she slowly walked toward the lectern. The applause stopped when she reached her destination, that's when the silence started. Joy was slowly searching a small patent leather purse for her glasses. I stopped breathing. Finding them, she then started looking for her note cards. We all watched as she found them and carefully laid them in a neat stack on the lectern.

From her first words, Joy's speech was understated elegance, my friends and coworkers were now on loan to her charisma. She neither used her glasses nor the notes and her fragile statute was replaced with energy, strength, and the most lovely grace as she recounted the past to create a new world for the young people in her audience. It was an amazing transition. I was breathing again.

After her talk, entertainment was provided by the Navy Sea Chanters who had several women in their chorus for the first time. We had cake and Joy was surrounded by admirers who shared their gratitude for a lifetime of inspiration to those she had affected in one way or another.

In reflection, I realized that this event was more important to her than the audience. Joy had led an exciting and glamorous life; there had been highs and lows. Self-made from the beginning, she had a sense of adventure and had pushed herself in many artistic, brave and creative directions. She had attended the State Department's Foreign Service Officer School; traveled extensively, written several popular travel books; and she had made wonderful contributions through her work as a civilian in the 1920s and 1930s with the old Bureau of Naval Aeronautics.

Following her retirement in 1953, she bought a plantation in the Virgin Islands and in an unladylike fashion climbed aboard a bulldozer to clear her land on terraced hillsides. One of the things she stood for was equality, her sense of social justice was complete and she spent a lifetime promoting parity between the genders.

We're all products of the people who influence us; Joy is one of the many personalities who altered my course of thinking.

International Women's Day

A few days ago, the United States celebrated International Women's Day. One of the speakers at UN ceremonies was Dr. Simar Samar, Afghanistan's Vice Chairman for Women's Affairs. Dr. Samar is another understated heroine we should applaud again and again for her many years of salvation to women's health and the education of girls.

Now she is the conscience of the third world encouraging us to support a war on poverty and rights for women and children.

It's a sad state of international affairs that disenfranchised people are not better protected. If you're poor, weak, or happen to be different from others in your neighborhood, country or region, you may be at peril. You may be killed in genocide, starved, or imprisoned.

We help the world become better for the downtrodden by publicly expressing intolerance for anything less that every human being having the basic universal rights of adequate food, shelter, health care, and educational opportunities; freedoms of choice in speech and religion; and equality of genders.

There are a lot of entitlements and responsibilities that come to us in the human family. The most important responsibility is caring for one another.

Freedom

Last week, The Honorable Nancy Goodman Brinker, Ambassador to Hungary, was interviewed by the BBC regarding her pride in Hungary's participation with the United States in fighting terrorism in Afghanistan and their opening of a trade office in Chicago, not far from her hometown.

A country of 10 million people with a 99 percent literacy rate, Hungarians are well educated and motivated; they love their families, liberty, and prosperity.

My first experience with Hungarians was in 1957 as Freedom Fighters and refugees fled Budapest as a result of their 1956 uprising against communism. The Soviet Union quickly moved to smother the disorder that protest brings and 35,000 people fled across borders to find refuge in safer parts of the world.

In my small hometown of Milan, Michigan, half a dozen young Hungarian men arrived and easily found work in the local foundry, which was owned by the Katona family. The Katonas were also of Hungarian descent.

Although these young men probably never saw themselves as ambassadors of their homeland, they left a lasting impression of decency, eagerness to learn, and a love of life.

In 1957, *Time* magazine honored little people who made a big statement by selecting Hungarian Freedom Fighters as their Man of the Year. Ironically, my new hometown, Herndon, Virginia, became the home of Ferenc Nagy in 1947. Mr. Nagy was the last freely elected premier

In Hungary before Russia dropped an iron curtain around Eastern Europe. Relocating to Herndon, he and his family enjoyed both a town home and a dairy farm in the country. The land mass of earth is enormous but the relationships we have in the global family are intimate as we learn to appreciate mutual values, in this case, freedom.

On March 14, admirers of Albert Einstein remembered his birthday. Born in 1879, Dr. Einstein was a lover of freedom who possessed one of the greatest minds of the 20th century. As a physicist, he proposed the theory of relativity, an assertion that light always moves in a straight line through empty spaces and always at the same speed in a vacuum, no matter what your vantage point.

From bombs to space travel, and electronics, the concept left his fingerprint on our daily lives. A 1922 Nobel Prize winner in physics, he was a Zionist, pacifist, and humanitarian who fled his native Germany where he felt his personal freedom threatened because of increasing dissonance between the Nazi government and its Jewish population. Albert Einstein is one of my heroes; not for his scientific merit, but for the way he used his prestige to promote freedom and a love of humanity in the international community.

I just finished reading a book about personal freedom; it is the classic, *The Power of Positive Thinking*, by Dr. Norman Vincent Peale. Dr. Peale initially published the book 50 years ago and since then it has sold over four million copies. It was recommended to me in 1980 as part of my orientation toward becoming a successful Navy recruiter.

On that first reading I hadn't trod on enough bumpy roads to understand the relevancy. This time around I found the volume enormously uplifting and Dr. Peale's concepts on mental attitudes to be a model for those who want to maintain strong faith, hope and optimism.

He wrote the book from his experiences as pastor at the Marble Collegiate Church in New York City where he and his staff taught creative living based on spiritual techniques. In his introduction to the book, he wrote, *by using the techniques outlined here....you will enjoy a delightful new sense of well-being.* There can be no doubt that if you could only have one book of ideas to improve your circumstances you'd want this one.

Dr. Peale discusses techniques for believing in yourself, expecting the best, relaxing, finding peace, and building constant energy.

Many of us are prisoners of negativity that we let misguide our judgments and peace of mind. In the book, Dr. Peale is a force for liberation of every reader who has issues that pull them down or hold them back. If you yearn for personal freedom, give this book a reading, my bet is you'll be glad you did.

San Diego, California

Last week I was in San Diego, California. As best I can determine, San Diegan's originated the greeting, *have a nice day!* San Diego's effulgent harbor and beaches have the bluest sky and waters, and the area's fresh, clean air contributes to positive spirits. Commuter traffic is less stressful; people are more calm and polite. They have a wonderful Spanish heritage combined with a large natural harbor that is one of the U.S. Navy's major ports. It is a Navy town filled with a patriotic citizenry: sailors, their families and retirees.

Local business chatter is focused on a San Diego company, Televator, which is installing 15-inch displays in the elevators of skyscrapers to provide a television-like experience while riding to the workplace's upper reaches. Besides the Televator, another workplace initiative is new legislation prohibiting pulling weeds by hand. The bill would enhance better working conditions in local fields where migrant workers spend their days bent over working in the soil. Agricultural employers would be required to provide long-handled hoes to ease back strain. Of course the landowners who hire migrant workers are claiming the pain of parting with the money to buy long-handled hoes is burdensome.

Speaking of pain, while staying at the Town and Country Convention Center in Mission Valley, I ran morning and evening up a steep hill on Ulric Street. The uphill course was a physical strain: lungs burned, heart raced, and my legs would become wobbly. The joy of this experience was that improvements were measurable from day-to-day; a reassurance that our human physical conditioning, just like our mental processes, can show impressive results in a relatively short time when there is a commitment to exercise.

There was also talk about the San Diego Padres and the prospects of their opening day game. It is spring, an interesting time of change in our natural and human worlds. In sports, we're starting baseball as we bid farewell to hockey and basketball. Muddy athletic fields are filling with kids, many are there for soccer practice but there are those who will be tossing around little white balls, some caught with big leather gloves. For those who like stories about kids and sports, you'll love this classic about a baseball game ten years ago at Wellington, Florida.

In the game there was a 7-year old first baseman, Tanner Munsey, who fielded a ground ball and then strained to tag a runner hightailing it from first to second base. Laura Bensen, the umpire, called the runner out. Tanner wasn't happy, he immediately went to Laura to say, *ma'am, I didn't tag the runner*. She reversed her decision sending the runner to second base. The little boy was awarded the game ball for his sportsmanship.

In another game, Laura was again the umpire and Tanner was playing shortstop. A similar play occurred and this time she ruled that the boy had missed the tag and the runner was safe at third base. The boy looked at the ump, and tossed the ball to the catcher. Sensing something was wrong; she asked Tanner, *did you tag the runner?* His reply, *yes.* Laura again reversed herself, calling the runner out. Of course, this caused an obstreperous coaching staff to challenge Umpire Benson who simply explained what had happened two weeks earlier. Her decree, *if a kid is that honest, I have to give it to him. This game is supposed to be for kids.*

My work in San Diego was as the master of ceremonies for a three-day symposium. On the second day, Bob Denend of Keyport, Washington, disclosed that his wife, Pat, had been courageously battling ovarian cancer, but received the prognosis a day earlier that her disease would be terminal. I asked our participants to remember Pat in their prayers. This request for prayer power for the comfort of Pat and her family also goes to you. Many of you pray often, others with less frequency, whatever schedule you use please include Pat Denend in your prayers.

Dallas, Texas

The lightning struck again and again from heaven to earth creating displays of artful light and power. The rains came and it flooded, but I missed the tornadoes and hail. Such is the story of a quick trip to Dallas, Texas, several days ago.

Dallas always leaves me in awe, it's an energetic place where people work hard, eat a lot, love the arts and shopping, and there is so much space. Big people live there, they have to be tough just to cope with the weather. Arriving at Dallas-Fort Worth Airport after dark on Sunday evening, I learned something new.

As a representative of the male species I've always thought it my duty to never consult road maps or ask for directions. To me, these seemed like fairly normal shortcuts to getting someplace quickly, but the truth is I've spent part of my life wandering around lost. But I am learning. In the stormy darkness of Dallas-Fort Worth, I easily became lost. This time it was different, I read a map; and asked directions on several occasions. Who says you can't teach old dogs a new trick? I found it remarkable how quickly my travels became more direct and efficient.

If you've never been to Dallas, you'll find four times more restaurants per person than New York City, the largest urban arts district and more shopping centers per capita than any other big city in America, and there are 82 Toastmaster Clubs.

My trip was at the invitation of The Susan G. Komen Breast Cancer Foundation to be part of a national task force whose members present their ideas on new directions in continuing the synergy of service to several million survivors, researchers, sponsors, supporters, and volunteers.

In attending our meeting I was reminded of the hard work, integrity, and keenly felt caring that characterizes those with The Komen Foundation. Their efforts save lives, it's as simple as that and they provide confidence that breast cancer as a life threatening disease will eventually be eradicated. Of interest, breast cancer mortality is declining, but the incidence of breast cancer cases is increasing; and least we forget, there will be an estimated 1,500 cases of breast cancer among men this year, 400 will die.

As the memory of travels to Texas fades, I want to mention Kay Presto of Ontario, California. Last week, I mentioned the value of reading and received some of the nicest responses. Kay wrote, *when I was 7, I took my mother by the hand and insisted that I get a library card from the library at the high school behind my house. I remember reading about nine books a week. On Saturdays, when I got old enough to walk there or go by bus, my mother would pack me a lunch, and I'd spend all day in the public library downtown, reading everything I could get my hands on during those hours. You are so right, books can take you anywhere in the world, and educate a person so much. To me, books are magical, and I truly appreciate your book review...*

What happened to the little girl who read books? Kay married Leon, had children and is a writer and broadcaster for Mutual Radio and ESPN, her specialty is auto racing.

Auto racing is literally the fast lane of journalism. A month ago, Kay rode in a two-seater Indy Race car at 160 mph, and in mid-March she sat in a racing 360 Modena Ferrari when it hit 180 mph. Besides her considerable accomplishments in journalism, she is a Distinguished Toastmaster, humanitarian, and a well-read woman of the world.

Bobby Leek

On April 12, 2002, I was privileged to be in the unique position of master of ceremonies for the retirement luncheon of Bobby Leek. Since 1988, he and I had worked together at the Naval Criminal Investigative Service in Washington. My simple MC duties were to set the stage and introduce 15 people who came forward to speak in homage for Bobby's character and the quality of his working life.

Speaker after speaker representing the Department of Defense, Central Intelligence Agency, General Services Administration and private enterprise presented gifts plus descriptions of his comradeship, leadership and technical competence.

Bobby is one of those small heroes who day-in, day-out do the right things over and over to make the world better. Retirements are part of the life cycle; we look forward to them with relish, but often regret the transformation when it arrives. Bobby seemed happy with future prospects and was justifiably proud of a productive working life.

In all, he spent 37 years serving America. As a sailor, he earned awards as a career counselor, served a tour in Vietnam and spent a winter in Antarctica. In his Navy civilian service, he developed three patents for security devices, wrote over 60 technical reports with enough merit that they were published, and responsibly managed programs worth more than 60 million tax-payer dollars.

We all know people like Bobby; they make our days and years better by creating harmony, don't ask for much, and eventually walk away to happy retirements. It's a cycle that seems to happen too quickly, if you blink and don't think about it, these wonderful people are gone without notice. Everything about being our best is honoring others; don't let important people in your life get away without presenting them an idea of their self-worth.

The Hyatt Regency's Tidewater Room, in Crystal City, Virginia, was the site of this heart-warming event. Thanks to his family and working friends Bobby now has a sense of his self-worth.

Changing the World

Some believe there is nothing one man or woman can do against the enormous array of world ills. Yet many of the world's great movements of thought and action have flowed from the work of a single person. A young monk began the Protestant Reformation, a young general extended an empire from Macedonia to the borders of the earth, and a young woman reclaimed the territory of France. It was young Italian explored who discovered the New World, and the 32-year old Thomas Jefferson who proclaimed that all men are created equal. These people moved the world, and so can we all.

Few will have the greatness to bend history itself, but each of us can work to change a small portion of events, and in the total of all those acts will be written the history of this generation. It is from numberless diverse acts of courage and belief that human history is shaped. Each time a person stands up for an ideal, or acts to improve the lot of others, or strikes out against injustice, he or she sends forth a tiny ripple of hope, and crossing each other from a million different centers of energy and daring, those ripples build a current that can sweep down the mightiest walls of oppression and resistance.

These are the words of Robert Kennedy to the young people of South Africa on their Day of Affirmation in 1966. Mr. Kennedy had a macro view of our contributions to one another in the global community; I see things in micro-sized pieces of one-on-one and small group relationships in homes, working centers, neighborhoods and churches.

When we are good examples, good teachers, generous givers, patient listeners or wise counselors, our acts go across oceans of humanity as one of the millions of tiny ripples that wash up against the world's negative thinkers. We positively influence a few people around us who affect others with the good thoughts that turn dark days to hidden rays of sunshine.

These ripples continue for generations because of you. It happens because you believe and live for the benefit of others. You're very important, without you there would be no one to read and appreciate Robert Kennedy's speeches, consider my humble opinions, or bring small improvements to an evolving world. We don't usually think of changing the world one person at a time, one day at a time, but that's the way little people go about their important work of making life better.

Enlightenment

Enlightenment is contained in books and conversations, churches, libraries, classrooms, and everyday situations. It comes from within, its truth, and can also be learned from our counselors, mentors and coaches.

Enlightenment is revelation, it tells us about our environment and how we adjust our attitudes to best fit. It is learning that there is unpredictability in human nature and the laws of nature. No two people are identical just as no two days with Mother Nature are ever the same. We adjust.

Enlightenment is learning that what you see isn't necessarily what you get. The poorest people are often the richest in their generosity to give of themselves and they may have the best personalities. People who have their well-being deeply threatened keep matters in best spiritual perspective.

Kids and the elderly are the best teachers of basic human values; they are also the most interesting and our true treasures. Angelic quality and brilliance exists in each of us just as there is a devilish nature. Enlightenment isn't always pretty; sometimes we learn something about ourselves that requires change for betterment. We don't like that much.

Change requires commitment, discipline and energy, there is risk of failure. We avoid failure, it's embarrassing. Enlightenment is learning by listening, not talking, it is also learned by experimenting, observing and thinking.

The right kind of thinking, positive, doesn't come easy. There is a darkish side to our nature that wants to dominate making negativity easier to apply.

Enlightenment is learning that time is our friend and our enemy. There probably will be a tomorrow to make up for today, but if we don't use our time well that day may be a repeat of the poor experience we had yesterday.

Recognizing our fallibility with humor is truth; people who understand the world laugh a lot. They promote humor with laughter at their weaknesses and in support of those around them. Laughing is important.

Enlightenment's trademark, *I understand*, is characterized by respect for our self and others. When we care, it shows. Taken a step further, it is most important to honestly say, *I understand how you feel*. That's called empathy. Empathy is the invisible thread that best connects the 6 billion people who inhabit earth. When we understand, we don't intentionally hurt one another and instead reach out to help.

Enlightenment is the richest inner quality; it shows in the charismatic warmth of our smiles, the merriment in our eyes, and a chin-up positive attitude. If you don't have it, you can get it. That's the beauty of enlightenment; it can come at any age, at any time.

Grassroots Politics

Standing erectly in my front yard is a red, white and blue sign that says, *Elect Bill Tirrell Mayor.* It's a nice little cardboard sign which is also posted on other lawns and along curbsides in Herndon, Virginia.

In off-year elections, communities in Northern Virginia typically have a ten percent voter turnout. That's too bad. Voting only takes a few minutes from normal routines and that is not much time to involve ourselves in the democratic process. Bill and other candidates for mayor and the town council also deserve better.

They are not much different from small town candidates anywhere else in America. Reading their community dossiers is like reading the markings on stepping stones to heaven. They have devoted most of their adult lives to serving others through leadership for good government, and voluntarism for the betterment of our kids and the elderly, fighting diseases, and generally taking good care of people.

Generalizing is a dangerous practice, but it is a safe bet that politicians are positive thinkers and at all levels they care deeply about their constituents. Logically, we should encourage them to be good in their service to us and express gratitude now and then for all they do. That involves voting. Voting is a personal responsibility, but also a personal joy in knowing that you're involved in the center of democracy by expressing choices.

The wisdom of choices is less important than exercising the right of choice. It is important to try for better or worse. Sometimes we won't make the right choice, that's okay; we tried by doing our best. That option is far superior to doing nothing, whether it's voting for a Bill Tirrell or taking better control of our lives.

Several days ago, Bill stopped by to say thanks for having the sign in my yard. I asked him to speak with my Indian neighbors next door. They had expressed a desire to meet him. Bill was wonderful and my neighbors thrilled. He talked a long time about wanting to visit India, they talked about loving America. That's grassroots politics-talking, listening, and caring about one another. The next step is voting on May 7.

Visiting Our English Cousins

Checking the speedometer, I was doing just about 80 mph. Looking back through rear view mirror; the two police cars both had pulsating blue lights. Furrowing my brow, I said to my travel mate, Les Vay, *you don't think they want me, do you?* Les said, *just to be safe, why not pull over?*

As it turned out that was sound advice. The British highway patrol did want me, not for speeding but because a good citizen had called in to say they thought I was driving while intoxicated. After the courteous officer told me that, I was at first stunned and then consumed with laughter. My problem wasn't strong drink or keeping up with the energetic flow of 80-90 mph traffic, but coping with a right hand steering wheel while driving in a left hand lane—just the opposite of the USA. After I went through a description of the challenges an American faces while driving in England, the officer nodded, smiled weakly, and wished us well.

That was my first interesting experience in visiting the mother country two weeks ago. This time my work took me to the coastal resort of Newquay (pronounced Newkey), which is located 275 miles southwest of London. Being a good listener and an ambitious reader is a solid basis for growth and learning, but please add to that formula the wonders of travel.

England is one of those garden spots of the world---lots of open, green space that brings humans close to the glories of nature; high rolling grassy hills with sheep, cattle and border collies; clouds, rain, wind, and cool temperatures; seacoasts with high cliffs, rolling surf, and large gulls that screech.

History is alive through stone gray castles and churches, time worn cemeteries, colorful medieval myths, and ancient mysteries such as Stonehenge, initially constructed 5,000 years ago for an unknown purpose. There are red double-deck buses, old-fashioned box-shaped black taxis, and sleek fuel-efficient European cars.

Fifty million people live in England, many of them carry umbrellas; they make 270 million annual visits to their community libraries, and consume 160 pints of spirits per capita. Even with gasoline at $4.50 a gallon, the British passionately love automobiles which they enjoy driving fast. They are also passionate about fish and chips, beef and vegetable pies, apple pie and cherry tarts, bangers (breakfast sausage) and mash, baked beans and bacon, goat cheese and tasty breads, and big salads with plenty of tomatoes.

You'll see an occasional McDonald's but don't plan on shopping at Wal-Mart. There are bed and breakfast Inns and hotels, many of them constructed hundreds of years ago. Their floors creak, there may be a draft or ghostly spirit, and sometimes you have to coax hot water faucets to deliver the goods.

With 43 clubs chartered under the auspices of Toastmasters' International, our English cousins are talkers. They are also generous. Following the 9/11 terrorist attacks in the US, Cornwall, the poorest county in England, donated about $60,000 to the families of lost police and firemen in New York City.

The BBC is the leading electronic media with BBC Radio organized around regional outlets such as the one at Cornwall. I listened to BBC Cornwall. That's where I heard the morning radio personalities, Pam Spriggs and Tim Hubbard, talk about Mrs. Bobbitt and her assistance to Mr. Bobbitt in launching his new career.

Pam and Tim were soon selecting their airwave words so carefully that neither could talk because of the laughter. As you may recall, several years ago in Virginia, Lorena Bobbitt, in a fit of uncontrolled anger, snipped off her husband's penis that was subsequently reattached by plastic surgeons. The unusual nature of the incident made national headlines; Mr. Bobbitt tried to capitalize on his name recognition by starting a new career in pornographic films. He never reached stardom and his new career ambitions soon fizzled. Later during my stay I learned that Lorena Bobbitt is a folk heroine in some circles of English sisterhood.

Besides working, I ran most mornings and evenings in cool temperatures on a coastal path beside rocky cliffs and sandy beaches. I met caring and smart people.

In conferring with Englishwoman Beverley Bowden, recreation and travel director at the Joint Maritime Facility, St. Mawgan, I explained that my room at the Glendorgal Hotel was not gushing with the hot water that I had come to appreciate in a morning shower. Beverley sweetly smiled before giving the soundest advice, *if our lives were all alike everywhere in the world, there would be little value or interest in travel.* I smiled and nodded agreement because I knew she was right, but never gave up my interest in a hot shower. Several days later, I figured out the facet setting which made my travel less of an adventure.

Since young adulthood, I have been a great admirer of our Native American heritage so you can imagine my delight at meeting Jeanne Eagle Bull, an Oglala Lakota Sioux from South Dakota. Jeanne was living in the small village of St. Mawgan with her husband, Jim Oxendine. Jim is a Lumbee Cherokee from North Carolina. While he serves the American Navy, she works as a civilian at the Joint Maritime Facility and attends nighttime college with the University of Maryland. The couple has two young sons, Jamison and Jacob, who busy themselves acquiring British accents.

Following this memorable week in England, I traveled to Greece, but that story is waiting for another day.

National Race for the Cure

Saturday, June 1, 2002, was an extraordinary day for 68,000 people in Washington, DC. Weatherwise it was hot and humid; peoplewise there was jubilation and optimism. The 13th annual National Race for the Cure again proved the power of moving positive people in the right direction.

Yes, there were really 68,000 registered walkers and runners for the 3.1 mile trek around the United States Capitol—the largest 5K run/walk on earth. It seems a minor miracle to find that many people in Washington, DC, who would agree on anything, but with the Race for the Cure there is not only agreement, but a strong social conviction that death from breast cancer must end.

Twelve to thirteen hundred volunteers supported the effort, that's where I was. The 100-people in the great crew I worked with passed out 75,000 bottles of Dasani water, and then we picked up all the empties and put them in dumpsters. This was a mighty thirsty crowd and the first year we've ever run out of bottled water. The energizing water team was composed mainly of people from the Young Marines, US Navy, and Toastmasters International.

All of this effort was the culmination of a year of planning and coordination by nearly a thousand people from Washington, Maryland, and Virginia to raise awareness to the importance of early detection of breast cancer and general funding for research, treatment and education. The momentum for the Race for the Cure Series is derived from another great crew, this one at The Susan G. Komen Breast Cancer Foundation in Dallas, Texas.

Since 1982, employees at The Komen Foundation have worked tirelessly to develop an infrastructure to support the ultimate end of breast cancer as a life-threatening disease. The Washington event is one of about 110 national and international Races for the Cure developed to spotlight the importance of finding a cure. After lung cancer, breast cancer is the second leading cause of death in women. Worldwide, 1.2 million women will contract breast cancer this year, in the USA that figure is 192,000. Some of these new breast cancer cases will involve 1,500 men, 400-500 will die.

There are hundreds of incredibly dedicated people who move me with their passion for this cause. Several that come to mind in fundraising are breast cancer survivors Vicki Martin Adamson, Connie Bash, and Patti Brownstein.

A few of the inspiring and hard working volunteers are Christine Cawayan, Theresa Clark, Pete Enchelmayer, John and Barbara Hunt, Renee Jones, Mike Kelley, Diane Mathis; survivors Rana Kahl, Kathy Mills, Ada Palmer, Larry Riley, Gwen Talbot, and George Scott.

This year's race had 760 teams, four of the best teams were organized by survivor Ernestine Ashley, newly retired from the Naval Space and Warfare Command; Jim Kelleher, National Geographic Society; Cindy Juvan, Deloitte Consulting; and Phyllis Wade, Naval Criminal Investigative Service.

If you can't read between the lines, I want to emphasize that these are fabulous people, who along with many others give off sparks with their enthusiasm for helping others. Ending the threat to life that breast cancer represents requires no less!

Blood Donation

Several weeks ago, I received a disappointing letter from Virginia's INOVA-Fairfax Hospital. It stated that the USDA had compiled new guidelines that might preclude me from donating blood or platelets.

Sure enough, my several years of living in Italy were considered disqualifying because beef imported from the United Kingdom might have been infected with mad cow disease. It's interesting how events in faraway lands manage to touch our lives in unexpected ways.

Since age 17, I've given more than enough blood to earn a 10-gallon donor pin and was two years into a new career donating platelets. With no age limit on blood/platelet donation I was looking forward to many more years of contributing.

The timing of the news couldn't be worse as the summer months bring blood shortages. About 75 million people who are eligible to donate blood in the US will not, America's blood needs are filled by the 4 million people who will donate, but they slack off with summer vacations.

There are 5,000 hospitals in the United States. In the past few days just one, INOVA-Fairfax Hospitals, did liver, lung, and kidney transplants as well as treated an emergency patient who needed 40 units of blood. Added to that, they currently have three premature babies each needing daily transfusions. Patients like these and their families rely upon our goodness to supply blood.

Blood is literally a life-giving fluid, which cannot be artificially duplicated. It has to come from another human being. In my view, people who care about people will overcome whatever fears, inconvenience or discomfort they may feel about donating blood. If you have read to this point, I hope you will consider donating blood soon by calling the American Red Cross or your nearest hospital to schedule an appointment.

Greece

There is a large body of land the size of Alabama that lies amidst the Aegean, Ionian and Mediterranean Seas. Along with the landmass, there are 2,000 islands that define Greece as sea and sky; it is an ancient country of adventurers, farmers, fisherman, poets, scholars, traders, warriors, and storytellers.

In 5,000 years, the Greeks have seen it all, they learned about the world's problems from Pandora who mistakenly opened her box to unleash chaos and havoc; Hippocrates became the Father of Medicine; and Homer wrote heroic stories.

Today, 10 million people live within sight of Mount Olympus, a 9,570-foot snow-covered giant that symbolizes a rugged land. The people there are readers and writers, their literacy rate is 95 percent; Greek Orthodox Is the religion of choice for 98 percent of the people; and tourism is the major industry. Several hundred thousand people (11 percent of the workforce) worry about the future because they are unemployed, their economy is relatively small.

They love cars, and on straight, level stretches of highway traffic rushes ahead at 80 mph in fuel efficient European cars. With gas at $3 a gallon, busses; trains, motorcycles and bicycles are popular, so is walking.

In late May, I was fortunate to learn firsthand about Greece during a working week at Larissa, a small community not far from the Aegean Sea.

Jogging most mornings and evenings along the Pinios River, I encountered a few fellow joggers and many walkers as we transverse paths lined with wildflowers. The dainty red poppy was most prominent among the trailside audience that stood with windblown grace nonchalantly watching over the human parade.

I reached the river and its park by jogging five minutes from the Metropol Hotel on narrow streets past strollers, outdoor cafes, shops, plazas with ornate fountains, and an ancient theater. The sounds, sights and smells of this journey were uplifting.

Nature's fragrances of jasmine, petunias, pansies, and red roses mixed with scents of perfume, freshly baked cinnamon baklava and lamb being slowly cooked for souvlaki. Church bells toll at 7 am and 7 pm throughout the city, some of the churches had been the site of miracles, passersby pause in reverence when near these monuments to man's greatest faith.

The one McDonalds in Larissa serves Greek burgers on pita bread and has a café with espresso and delicate pastries. I met interesting people. Old men sat on park benches discussing a changing world; younger men sat at outdoor cafes sipping their beverages while watching women pass; women sat at tables sipping their drinks and watched male strollers.

After Greek, major languages are English and French; however, Larissa is off-the-tourist path with the result that relatively few people speak English. I was reminded again of the power of a smile in connecting with positive people who will figure out one way or another how to communicate.

Finding new friends is like striking gold, particular far from home. During the week I became close to Sakis, Dora and Nicoli Zerdali. They are proprietors of Sakis Café at the post office plaza. The Zerdali family had lived and worked on Long Island, New York for 15 years. While there they did what they do best, operate a family restaurant. With growing children and the tug of old friends and family, they returned to Greece five years ago to open two restaurants.

Nicoli's love is music, a passion he pursued fervently in America. Now in Greece, he is disappointed with the opportunities to follow the urges that drive artistic people. In our conversations, he told me something that stuck, *when you've lived in the United States, you'll never be fully satisfied living anywhere else.*

For the safety of her two small children, Dora is grateful for the low crime rate in Greece, but worries about an encroaching drug culture. And Sakis, he is happiest of all because he loves the food business. Meeting the Zerdali family and many others during a week in Greece was another lesson in learning that we truly are all related regardless of our language, culture or geographic situation. The theme of this experience is that if we let differences become isolating barriers to appreciation, understanding and respect for one another, we miss the enrichment that best defines humanity.

Presbyterians

Church membership brings a comforting affiliation with the beauty of stained glass, the uplifting spirit of song, and a shoulder-to-shoulder solidarity with those who have faith, hope and optimism—my three favorite beliefs.

In America and all over the world we either believe in a higher power or seek links to validate spirituality. If you think I am kidding, you should know that there are over 4,200 different religions, churches, dominations, religious bodies, faith groups, tribes, cultures, and movements in the world. Through circumstances of birth and parental influence, I am a Presbyterian. In the United States, there are 5.5 million of us in over 20,000 congregations. My community of faith is the Trinity Presbyterian Church in Herndon, Virginia

Trinity has 800 members who perform good works as missionaries helping the elderly, poverty stricken, and those suffering from disease and hunger. We are typical of those in other religions in that we care deeply about humanity—children and the elderly are highly respected as they should be.

The Presbyterians are a family of spirit who cry, eat, sing, laugh, and pray together. When people become sad, lonely, or scared they are compelled to join the company of their fellow beings for comfort and strength. Many find faith, hope and optimism, but some miss the point.

Following last September's terrorism attacks at the World Trade Center and Pentagon, houses of worship overflowed; there were not enough pews or folding chairs to seat everyone; however, as anxiety levels lowered, attendance diminished.

Several studies in the past few years suggest that about 40 percent of the people in America attend church irregularly or not at all and attendance might be declining. Other studies more optimistically state that attendance is increasing. Regardless of the trends or what the masses believe or do, I know that involvement with good people brings out our best qualities. Finding yourself in a community of the faithful is an easy and convenient means of discovering more about yourself and those around you.

All of us possess exceptional personal qualities; we're highly intelligent and have an unlimited capacity for compassion, generosity and love. But there are barriers to being our best—for starters there is a lack of self-knowledge, belief in our abilities, and trust in one another.

Sadly, after we reach adulthood society does not proactively reach out to nurture the qualities that we need to grow. As captains of our destiny, we're required to design our own lives. Many people have done well in this personal artistry; you can see the aura of serenity that supports their happiness and satisfaction. Others are behind.

If you're one of those who feels detached from where you should be, there is a world of opportunity waiting. Opportunities for change through personal growth have never been greater than they are today.

One of the most convenient and positive life experiences is inside the houses with stained glass windows, uplifting spirits and shoulder-to-shoulder solidarity—a place where you're always welcome.

Touched by Grace

Through a turn of good fortune, June 20, 2002, developed to be one of my most enjoyable days of the year. Several weeks earlier, I had been asked to serve as master of ceremonies for the retirement luncheon of my friend Grace Hill and her coworker LaNita Jones. Both ladies were retiring from 30-year careers in Federal service as equal opportunity specialists.

Their final years were spent at the Navy's human resource office in Washington. Over 40 friends and family members gathered at the *Market Street Restaurant* in Southwest Washington for an event that popped the top on the barometer of human warmth.

Vincent Vacarro, Ph.D, director of the human resources officer was the day's featured speaker. In his remarks, Dr. Vacarro spoke eloquently and with appreciation for the contributions of Grace and LaNita in their pioneering efforts to bring respect and understanding to Navy work centers.

Earl Matthews, a representative of the union and Blacks in Government, next took the lectern to praise Grace for the excellence of her contributions to a variety of volunteer organizations at the Washington Navy Yard. In the *This is Your Life* segment, guests stood to speak from the heart for Grace and LaNita. The first speaker was Sylvester Simpson, LaNita's father, who described his daughter's beauty and support to their family. Mr. Simpson was followed by Jim White, Joyce Battle, Katharine Jackson, Loretta Johnson, Ruby Johnson, Tyrone Hill, Veda Lewis, Linda Simpson, and Karen Smith.

Next on the program were gifts of balloons, bouquets of roses, more hugs, and additional laughter. Grace and LaNita had the last word in thanking the assemblage and describing their positive feelings about retirement. Neither woman was observed to shed crocodile tears at the prospect of starting new lives. They reflected in the spirit of *I wouldn't take a million dollars for the experience, but wouldn't give you a nickel for another day!*

What made this such a fabulous experience was the generous outpouring of affection for two people who worked hard to make things better for others. They deserved the praise and more.

One-room Schoolhouses

Last week, I drove across Maryland, Pennsylvania, and Ohio to reach my boyhood home in Southeast Michigan. Looking across the countryside there are three things that standout about our American heritage: white country churches with prominent steeples, old weather-beaten barns, and boarded-up one-room school houses.

I love those sights when the vista offers rolling fields of wheat or corn, pastures with cows, and patches of forest here and there. It all reminds me of our nation's faith, industry, and solidarity from years ago when communities prayed together, worked together, and optimistically believed that their children would fare better in life than they did. Parents still believe that, it's today's grown children who have doubts.

Although I enjoy the sights, sounds and smells of country, the institutions one finds there are most important. Take one-room school houses for instance. I am an expert on those wonderful monuments to country-style learning. From the first through the sixth grade, I attended the Heath School with 30 other kids. Most of those years, we studied under Mary Farrar, an elderly woman whose affectionate nature was challenged by the shenanigans of little, medium, and big-sized kids bringing life to one large room.

Eighty years ago, America had nearly 200,000 one-room school houses. Today there are only about 325. Michigan has 21 remaining, but Heath isn't one of them. It was closed about 1955 in favor of a consolidated school where children were bused to classes morning and evening; a few years later Heath School burned to the ground.

Montana and Nebraska have the most one-room schools and California is the only state that is seeing an increase. Out there they are called one-teacher schools. It seems that as the Internet allows more parents to work in remote country settings, their kids are experiencing limited opportunities for a public education. Taking an old idea and making it new, California is constructing little schools in the country.

I liked my early education and wouldn't trade the learning environment for anything. There were spelling bees every Thursday, we sang through music class broadcast on a Monroe County radio station on Fridays; there were holiday programs, generous recesses; and most of us had rotating responsibilities to sweep the floor, empty trash, clean the blackboard, carry coal for the stove, or help the smaller children. We also rang the school's bell to signal the start of school, return from recess and reconvening after lunch.

Two pictures hung on the wall, one was of Abraham Lincoln, and the other was the father of our country, George Washington. We said the Pledge of Allegiance each morning while facing a large American flag.

Although a straight A student, I didn't feel much like a scholar and after transferring to the large consolidated school at Milan my grades plummeted. Today, modern testing devices indicate that kids fare better in the small, multi-class settings.

The purpose of my drive to Michigan was to transport and install my father's new computer and then help him learn how to use it for e-mail. The effort was flawless. Can Larry Welch, Sr., send and receive e-mail with ease? Not really, but he is enthusiastic to learn a little bit more every day. That guarantees his ultimate success.

At 80, dad knows the importance of feeding brain cells new ideas. It's a shame that people at every age can't apply this simple concept to expand their thinking power.

Besides computer talk with dad, there was a family outing, picnicking with a dozen classmates, attendance at Saline's First Presbyterian Church, reading, and a dizzying experience with *The Spider Man* movie. My grandnephew David, 8; and nieces Ashley Anne, 6; and Erin, 3, proved themselves again to be great kids rushing too quickly to adulthood.

During this Fourth of July week, our focus is on patriotic blessings and grace. We are the most fortunate country on earth; there has never been another society with more advantages for its people. Just like you, I am thinking of the sacrifices that brought America independence and rejoicing in the freedoms of religion, speech, press and choice. My thoughts are also on the blessings of family and friends, white country churches, old barns and scholarship in country schools.

Links in a Chain

These are exciting times, but to keep up we'll need to buckle our seat belts and stay positive. The world is on an emotional roller coaster with daily surprises that shouldn't be so surprising. A mass fear is affecting Americans as they bail out of corporate faster than summer lightning. If the trend continues, interest rates, inflation, tax revenues, international trade, and global employment will be seriously affected.

Should the worse happen, don't be surprised if we adjust and survive just fine. In remarks last week, Federal Reserve Chairman Alan Greenspan spoke of the infectious greed of corporate America. No surprise there!

Ohio Congressman James Traficant is taking a turn as our national clown. He's missing the bulbous red nose and huge floppy shoes, but his big mouth and small brain makes up for the difference. I know Pam Spriggs and Tim Hubbard at BBC Radio Cornwall are having lots of fun with their listeners over Traficant's quirky behavior.

The export of American humor can't help but promote international brotherhood. I had been concerned about the trade imbalance of humor as we were enjoying more laughs at British expense than they were mining from us. Thanks to Congressman Traficant, we're back in balance.

AIDS/HIV continues to take a horrible toll in America and elsewhere. Unless dynamic leadership and a world commitment to compassion evolve to combat this scourge, several countries in Africa may cease to exist in 10-15 years. The Palestinians are questioning the value of suicide bombers. They are reflecting on what the terrible toll in human life and suffering has really accomplished. Israelis are wondering about the value of their occupation on the West Bank. They are also asking: *What have we accomplished?*

Iran and the United States are working harmoniously on the construction of roads and schools in Afghanistan. *The Wall Street Journal,* friends, family and freedom lovers are thinking of reporter Daniel Pearl as his murderers are sentenced in Pakistan. Zimbabwe's President Robert Mugabe continues to harass journalists to stifle freedom of speech. The President and his government are crooked and inept; they think muffling the new media will change their image. They may also think the world is flat!

The point here is that we humans are all connected like links in a chain. The skin color varies, religions vary, sexes are different, we don't all like the same foods or speak the same language, but we are identical in feelings. We all want and feel happiness, satisfaction, and security in our lives. We want our kids to succeed, we want to love and be loved, and we think about issues of fairness.

Because of technology, global economics and our human relationships, what happens to someone 10,000 miles away eventually affects us in one manner or another. The needless loss of a life will cause us to mourn or become more fearful, the exposure of fraud makes us skeptical and less trusting. We also become inspired to laugh or feel pride when a friend makes the right remark or a world leader courageously takes a stand for humanity.

Obviously, recent weeks have brought challenges to our faith, hope and optimism, but that's exactly where we want to remain. Giving in to fear of the future, caring less about one another, or letting anyone affect our pride in humanity is a step into the shadows. Our clowns, criminals, and those influenced by infectious greed are dark figures we see from the lightness of our being.

Our grace is a reflection of faith. Trading faith for fear, becoming resentful or angry, or losing our sense of humor is not the territory that positive thinkers spend time exploring.

Ginny Kibler

If you're like me you have days when you're slogging through goop, sometimes not sure of your destination and the worthiness of the journey. Then someone from your family or a friend gives a word of recognition, encouragement or inspiration; your back straightens, your footing becomes more solid, and the obvious becomes clear: everything will be okay. That happens to all of us again and again as our best relationships flourish with quality results. Friends and family help us realize our high value, keep us on track, give us resolve, and make us laugh.

I was reminded of the platinum value of supportive friends one evening two weeks ago. Ginny Kibler and I had a reunion dinner at *Jordan's* in Washington. As I listened, it came to mind that Ginny is one of those passionate, smart people who possesses an abundance of positive energy, a gift she graciously shares.

I hadn't seen Ginny in 18-months, but through the blessings of the Internet we'd exchanged notes now and then. Since meeting seven years ago, we had worked together coaching people in Toastmasters International, feeding the homeless at Martha's Table, and helping Komen's Race for the Cure in Washington and Baltimore

Besides her compassion, I've been most impressed with Ginny's brain, she's smart enough to have earned three college degrees, has already read more books than I will in my lifetime, became one of Uncle Sam's senior economists, attended flight school, and has earned designation as a Distinguished Toastmaster.She's an excellent speaker, listener, leader, follower, learner, and an avid globetrotter. Under pressure, she's calm, cool and decisive.

I am fortunate to know Ginny, she's one of my most loyal friends, and sets the right kind of example. In her work at the Environmental Protection Agency, she developed an economic model for the 21st century to better understand the cost-benefits of preserving natural resources. She's proud of that and rightly so, we need these models to help everyone understand the importance of balancing environmental concerns with our human nature.

Coincidentally, Ginny and I started flight school at the same time in 1997. Neither of us knew the other was even interested in aviation. As we later compared notes, I found that Ginny's student pilot days were a lot more exciting than mine. She flew faster airplanes and her instructors were more flamboyant. Her descriptions of their cartoonish mannerisms often made me laugh. Now and then she also related heart in your throat descriptions of practice stalls, unpredictable crosswinds, and simulated emergency landings. One of these adventures bears repeating.

On November 17, 1998, Ginny took off from the airport at Manassas, Virginia, for a solo cross-country flight to Newport News and return. This was her second long cross country trip and one of the final requirements in qualifying as a private pilot. Although she may have violated airspace around Richmond, there was a beautiful landing at Newport News. After refueling, she took off for return to Manassas. One of the navigation dangers that pilots face is getting lost. To avoid that embarrassing outcome many pilots follow railroad tracks, rivers and highways.

As she followed a highway toward Tappahannock, Virginia, Ginny noticed that the engine was making strange sounds. Her first thought, *OK, it's the engine working hard.* At Tappahannock she changed course for Brooke, Virginia, and that's when she smelled something burning. Calling Dulles Airport on her radio, she told them she was a student pilot, had an overheated engine, needed directions to the nearest airport, and might need fire equipment standing by.

They gave her a 270-degree heading toward Shannon Field at Fredericksburg, five miles away. The airspace around Shannon cleared for what was expected to be an emergency landing. Setting up her landing in this stressful situation, she came in too low over a grove of trees, gave the engine power to avoid losing more altitude and crashing, but then forgot to power back until she'd used half of the short runway.

Touching down on one wheel, she braked hard; the plane skidded and bounced over to the other wheel, she applied more full brakes, tires smoked. The plane stopped in an overrun area 10-feet from a passing train.

Turning the plane around, she taxied back to the runway and then to the general aviation building, she shut the plane down, opened the canopy and burst into tears in front of eight men standing there waiting for her arrival. She described the tears this way: *I am sure Amelia Earhart never cried.* Smiling, Ginny ended the story with a question: *So, Larry, wanna fly with me?* That's Ginny, a high flying friend who finds humor almost everywhere.

Kids

On my street in Herndon, Virginia, the summer has been a time of discovery as kids spend lazy days enjoying the company of one another. They are growing up.

I smile in wonder at what they will become given their starts in life. A group of 5-7 year half-pints stop by most days. They know my freezer is filled with iced treats, and to get one all they have to do is tell me a credible story of how good they've been that day.

In cases of doubt, they know I'll ask questions just to get all the facts straight. I also get collaborative testimony from playmates in their group. Because of her age, 2-year old Sanya can't talk well enough to tell me how good she has been, her mother has to do that. And as it turns out her behavior isn't perfect. She likes to pinch her boyfriend, Jay, age 3. Jay doesn't like being pinched, he cries. Sanya then hugs and kisses him, and then they both start laughing. The other day, she inadvertently dialed 9-1-1 when her parents weren't watching. When the police arrived to check out the mystery call, Sanya smiled and blew them a kiss.

Ten months ago, in Monroe, Michigan, my grandnephew David Nichols, 9; and grandnieces Ashley Nichols, 7, and Erin Nichols, 3, created small bags of red, white and blue candy, and carrying an American flag they went door-to-to door selling the candy. They collected $220 for victims of 9/11.

During the past school year, my 10-year old daughter Mary became the top classroom kid in giving presentations. She combined creativity in the design and use of props with a passion for speaking in front of others.

Not everyone loves our kids, there are adults who exploit, kidnap, assault, sell drugs to, starve, and torture children. Parents ruin self-esteem, confidence and the trust kids put into the adult world with verbal and physical abuse. Children bring us to tears with their bravery while suffering from chronic and fatal illnesses.

In third world countries kids are dodging bullets and land mines, don't have clean water, suffer from malnutrition, lack basic medical care, and some are starving to death. How bad is it? Roger Moore of James Bond fame has been the goodwill ambassador to UNICEF since 1991. This is what he said: *When I started working with UNICEF, one of the statistics I saw was that 40,000 children die every day from preventable diseases, such as measles, tetanus, and diphtheria. The latest figures show that the number is down to 29,000, this gives me a certain sense of satisfaction---to know that our efforts make a difference.* Which one of these millions of kids that die every year would be the one to lead us to world peace, discover the cure for an incurable disease, or devote their lives to the service of God?

None of us can do it all to save and protect children, but we do have a responsibility to do what we can. Doing what we can may require inconvenience as we donate time and attention to kids or dig into wallets and purses to send dollars in nurturing directions. We can also help children read better; help teachers in the classroom or assist in Sunday school; coach youth athletics; help single-parents with encouragement, time, and money; or become involved with a special children's project.

Connie Bash of Alexandria, Virginia, recently asked me to check out the web site Team-Ethan.org as a special interest project. On the same day, Rana Kahl of Manassas, Virginia, wrote about another opportunity to help by suggesting that I visit www. msnusers.com/jonathansjourney. I did and recommend both sites to you, particularly with the idea that they are projects you can become involved with that make a valuable contribution to the kid's community, doesn't take much time, and might only cost you a few dollars.

In the case of Connie's referral, Team-Ethan focuses on pediatric brain tumors. Ethan Gumabay, a native Virginian who looks to be about three years old, was initially diagnosed with his brain tumor on May 4, since then he has had a major operation and is now receiving chemotherapy. Brain tumors are the second most common cancer in children behind leukemia.

At team-ethan.org, you can learn more about what happens to kids with brain tumors, check into the bake sale in Reston on August 18; and the bike ride in Columbia, Maryland on September 15. These are events to raise funds and awareness to the dangers of brain tumors in children.

Jonathan Dzury, hailing from Columbus, Ohio, is a patient at the children's cancer center at Johns Hopkins Hospital. He was diagnosed with acute myeloid leukemia on April 30. At 2-years of age, Jon is undergoing a four month hospital stay away from home for initial chemotherapy. Visit his web site, visit him in the hospital, and learn how you can become involved in his cure.

Ethan, Jon and other kids are the future. We want them to be strong, smart, healthy, confident, and compassionate. They will get that way because we're their benefactors, coaches, care-givers, and positive examples. From experience I know at least half the people in the world are candlesnuffers. They aren't going to support much of anything and will discourage the rest of us. We should all want to be known as people who light candles and resist giving in to such nonsense from the darkside. Check out team-ethan.org and www.msn.users.com/johnathansjourney, see what you think!

Can you light a candle?

Reading for Lifetime Riches

Motivational speaker and author Charles *Tremendous* Jones made one of the truest statements you'll ever hear when he said, we will be the same person five years from now that we are today except for the books we read, the people we meet and the places we visit.

Never changing is fine, many people don't. My grandfather, William Clay Aper, wasn't much for change. He lived in isolation on a small farm in Michigan. His work involved soil, weather, and animal husbandry; his socialization was family; and his recreational pursuits were fishing, listening to baseball games on the radio, reading the newspaper, and drinking wine. He was hard working and from his inner glow I'd say he was elated to live life on those terms.

Times have changed since my grandfather's days on the farm, we are far better educated and we no longer live and work in agricultural settings. We live in cities and towns near our offices in complicated relationship with friends and family where we experience the challenges of on-the-job competition made more difficult by the stress of making ends meet.

Every day the world changes, with each passing day, the rate of change increases. Ideally, we are keeping pace with the world by learning and growing from reading, meeting people and traveling. But many of us are not living ideally or even putting forth the effort to keep up.

In an article on attitude that appeared in a recent issue of *Messages from the Masters* (Jun 28, '02), Jerry Clark stated that research shows 58 percent of high school graduates never read another book from cover to cover the rest of their adult life and that about 78 percent of the population has not been in a bookstore in the last five years.

The National Adult Literacy Council says that 50 million Americans read at the 4th or 5th grade level and that reading failure in our country is at an epidemic proportion. Because of the lifetime riches I have discovered in books, I grieve for those who can't or won't read. Humorist Will Rogers could be a serious philosopher. One of his pearls of wisdom was, *people only learn through two things. One is reading and the other is association with smarter people.*

A disciplined pattern of reading brings knowledge that motivates us in positive directions. Just as a fast-moving streak of lightning reveals mysteries of a dark summer sky, reading creates explosions of insight as we come to realize who we are and where we should be going. All reading boils down to learning about ourselves and others. Whether you read biographies, novels or dig into books on history, philosophy, psychology, gardening, or a hard science, you will learn about yourself and others. You'll learn to appreciate and respect talent, your own as well as others; you'll become less fearful of a world that intimidates with its complexity and wonder; you'll become more confident in whom you are becoming; and you'll care more about the world. Besides the personal growth and the joy of learning, you'll be well entertained.

If you're not now a reader, you can start by disciplining yourself to read as little as 15-minutes a day. Soon, and this is my promise to you, these small regular intervals of reading will be the favorite time of your day. Or you could take a round-the-world cruise, making new friends among the smart set. Nice choices, but you can make mine reading, it's more practical and probably more fun to boot!

Aching Hearts, Positive Action

The current statistics on suicide are staggering. For every two homicides in America, there are three suicides. Every hour and forty-five minutes another young person commits suicide. Suicide is the second leading cause of death among college students and the third-leading cause among youth 15-24 years old.

The trend is horrible. Since 1970, the teen/youth suicide rates have tripled. Chrissie Carrigan, 15, took her own life nearly a year ago, and the family is remembering her as more than a statistic.

On Saturday, November 9, 2002, they have organized a 2-mile walk at Northwest High School, Germantown, Maryland. Besides raising awareness to the dangers of teen suicide, the walk is a fund raiser for a scholarship fund to be awarded at Northwest High School. Registration is $15, and includes a free t-shirt. Organizers are also asking walkers for donations and any other funds they can raise. There will be random drawings and prizes will be awarded. Checks should be payable to the Chrissie Carrigan Memorial Fund, and mailed to Kathie Carrigan, 12448 Quail Woods Drive, Germantown, Maryland 20874.

Kathie was Chrissie's mother; Chrissie was also sister to walk organizers Peter Colwell and Trevia-Lynne Carrigan.

Paula Emerick of Seattle, Washington, was among 2,858 walkers who recently completed the Seattle Avon Breast Cancer 3-Day Walk. More that a stroll around the block; Paula stepped out smartly through 60-miles of what she termed *excitement, empowerment, positivity, kindness and emotion.*

Long identified as one of life's champions, Paula dedicated her walk and fund raising commitment to her mother Myrna, and stepmother Margaret, who both passed as victims of cancer. Ninety-four donors generously gave $7,290, with Starbucks matching an additional $700 in donations from her coworkers. For training, Paula walked 345 miles in four months.

Thinking of those who live with high purpose, it's impossible not to be exceedingly proud of those whose aching hearts lead to positive actions.

Lessons in Living

I was fortunate to earn a college degree. It came later to my life than most; I didn't wear the cap and gown of university graduation until 1995.

The courses I loved most were English composition and literature, geology, music, law, economics, human relations, accounting, statistics and marketing. There were no courses that I disliked. I also noticed that there were no courses in street smarts, but sometimes there were lessons that tended toward that direction.

The first street smart lesson I learned in economics was that the great challenge of our world is how to fulfill unlimited wants and needs with limited resources. There is only so much money to go around.

The second lesson was that for every person in our society who is over compensated for their labors, there is at least one who is underpaid. Think about CEOs, movie stars, and professional athletes who are taking home many millions annually. CEOs now draw about 500 times the salary of those on the factory floor. They may be great at what they do, but to get the idea here compare them with a teacher, paramedic, or policeman who may also be great at what they do. Unless you're a CEO you'll sense the inequity.

My third lesson in economics was derived from living: *There is no such thing as a free lunch.* We've heard that so often we seldom even give it a second thought. It means that we get back what we invest in ourselves and our environment through hard work. That can take many forms. To me it means being authentic; honest with ourselves and everyone else; improving personal and professional skills, treating others with respect, kindness and understanding; being disciplined; and not taking ourselves too seriously. The things I've just mentioned don't have anything to do with money. They have everything to do with being happy and how we interrelate with others. This all fits comfortably under the banner of social intelligence.

I like to refer to social intelligence as *street smarts*. This is the intellect we don't learn in a classroom, it comes through deliberate soul searching, thinking about what we see and hear, listening to ourselves, and thinking about how we can get along better. In short, it's being tuned in to our human environment. Remember Clara Peller? In 1984, Clara, an octogenarian at the time, affected Wendy's economically with her three word question, *where's the beef?*

A Chicago widow who had been born in Russia, Clara's loudly voiced inquiry caused Wendy's sales to skyrocket 31 percent; profits were up 24 percent for the year in which her television ad appeared. In our case, we might ask, *where's the happiness?*

The obvious answer is that it's inside us, it's not inside your wife, your husband, your girlfriend, children, your boss, or your neighbor. It comes from your core being, happiness is not part of the great economic challenge, happiness is not rationed, and an infinite number of people can be as happy as they choose. The theme *where's the happiness* can have a lot to do with not expecting a free lunch as well as being fairly compensated for life's labors. It's also about being responsible for our own well being and not relying on a boost from those around us. As they say in China, *man who wait for roast duck to fly into mouth, have very long wait.* That has nothing to do with economics either.

Opal Mae Aper

It is now officially fall, but the leaves won't be as purplish or red as usual in many parts of the United States because of drought conditions. Kids have now been back in school long enough to recall that socializing with so many friends everyday comes with the price of doing homework. In my unofficial survey at the local peanut gallery, the odds that a child actually wants to get up early and head off to school has dropped from 100 percent to 50 percent in the past four weeks.

Our temperatures are mercifully cooler, pansies and chrysanthemums are out in dazzling color, and Librans are all smiles because this is their birthday time.

On October 4, my grandmother would have been 110 years old. Opal Mae Beeker was born in 1892 in a little white farmhouse near Tippecanoe, Indiana.

The Beeker family was of German pioneering stock, people who had settled and resettled America since the 1750s. They had struggled as patriots, traded with Indians, broken prairie sod, fought to preserve the Union, and worked hard at hanging on. Her family history is among the many millions of colorful threads that weave the cloth of our unique American experience.

In 1910, she married Will Aper, my grandfather. Three children were born of this loving union; my mother arrived in 1923, born in the same modest farmhouse as her mother years earlier.

As the daughter, wife, and ultimately the mother of farmers, Grandma Aper toiled from before dawn until after dusk maintaining a home and helping with farm chores. She was a time manager, proficient cook, and generous in her spirit. Anything she had, she was willing to share. Although her life was difficult, she was positive, laughed often, and cherished her family.

Her one failing; she was a poor driver. Being behind the wheel didn't dampen her curiosity and chatty nature and that was her downfall. She tended to look at those with whom she was speaking, at other times her blue eyes roamed the roadside landscape. Because her hand-eye coordination was different from many, the car would gradually drift into the direction that she was looking. If she was watching the road, there were no problems.

A fairly conservative fellow who maintained a calm, serene nature, my grandfather would neither drive an automobile nor ride with her if there were alternatives. My sister Linda and I, being kids, didn't have a choice, we rode when told. Because of circumstances our survival instincts surfaced at an early age as we watched the country roads and often gave grandma a nudge to get her attention back on driving. Her typical response was to laugh in masking embarrassment and do self-talk, *I'd better watch where I'm going!* Linda and I would sometimes look at another, grin slightly, and nod in agreement.

If you haven't recently thought about those who influenced your nurturing and what that might mean, fall is the time to do it. We are caught in nature's passage between two extremes, a hot dry summer and what may be a cold, snowy winter. During this transition, it's good to give thought to where we started, where we're at, and where we're going.

I've had thousands of positive influences in my life, each bringing the exertion of an exemplary person who shared his or her values in one good example after another. I remember my grandmother at this time because she was an early and wonderful part of my life. She was highly sociable and loved reading. Part of me is her; it's now my responsibility just like it is yours to be a positive person who exemplifies the good behavior brought to us by others.

Faithful and cheerful people who made our world better also handed us a torch to light tomorrow's path of optimism. We need one another for this source of validation to expand our frame of reference. Without exception, everyone has a collection of unique gifts and talents that no one else in the world possesses.

By modeling respect, patience, persistence, honesty, and understanding, we inspire others, there's no getting around it. It isn't always easy and we won't always be successful, but it should be everyone's quest. Personally, I'd like to be a better example of good driving behavior, but with a grandmother like mine that's a bit difficult.

Birthday Reflection

Last Saturday (October 5) was my birthday and as birthdays go, it was a fine day. I did just about what I do every Saturday: worked around the house, read, reflected, jogged, and enjoyed those around me.

The day may have been a little different in that people were more pleasant; however, that assessment may be influenced by the inner glow I had at being alive to kick off another year.

Life has been a charmed experience for me, almost magical in a sense. When I reflect on my past, I remember an extensive supporting cast composed of loving people: parents, grandparents, aunts and uncles, sisters, cousins, teachers, ministers, coaches, children, school mates and childhood pals who long ago graduated to the category of oldest and dearest friends.

When we're young, we're stuck with the adults around us; they may be kind, wonderful and wise individuals; or something less. As we grow, we learn to make choices into which people we will put our trust. We try to make good choices, but invariably there are mistakes. Most of us are fortunate to have fabulous people around us. These individuals give their valuable time, the right kind of attention, understanding, and encouragement. They are also nonjudgmental.

I am often complimented as being one of the most positive people on earth and that's humbling. The real credit goes to those who helped me as a kid and the sea of mankind that surrounds me today. What these people did for me and probably do for you is create the foundation from which we continue to build our character, spirituality and personality. If we get a good start in life, it follows that we'll push forward to educate ourselves, develop a sense of service, and expand our horizons.

Birthdays are a personal New Year, more than celebration; birthdays should also be a time to give gratitude for life's blessings and also to think about tomorrow. We know that the future will be unpredictable; we can't control it, but we can control ourselves and that is our day-to-day stability. No matter what happens in the world, we can be positive and keep our birthdays memorable.

I hope yours is just as happy!

Ferenc Nagy

October 23, 2002, marks the 46th anniversary of the Hungarian Uprising. In 1956, hundreds of thousands of Hungarians took the streets to protest communist dictatorship. The revolt was crushed. By December, thousands of refugees were streaming across international borders to escape punishment.

Hungarians inspire me as a brave, smart and hard working people! One of the best was Ferenc Nagy. With just a 6th grade education, Mr. Nagy raised himself to become the last freely elected premier of Hungary before the iron curtain fell on Eastern Europe.

Every day wasn't perfect for him. In 1944, he was a prisoner of the German Gestapo, nearly dying in an aerial bombing of Budapest. Three years later as the Hungarian premier, while on vacation in Switzerland, the communists kidnapped his 5-year old son. Because of his popularity with the people, the communists needed a discreet way of removing him from Hungary's political spectrum.

Their shadowy offer was to exchange the boy for Mr. Nagy's resignation and exile. The swap was soon made on the Swiss border. He, his wife, and five children migrated to the United States where they settled in Virginia.

During exile his patriotic light never dimmed as he continued to remind the world that people who love democracy and freedom lived in Hungary. Although he died in 1979, there are a lot of people who remember his example of faith, hope and optimism. I know how gratifying it must have been for his family when, in 1989, the Iron Curtain was lifted and Hungary was allowed to pursue its highest and best destiny as a free state.

Freedom is a precious gift brought to us through the heroics of people like Ferenc Nagy, a high principled Hungarian who did his best under difficult circumstances.

South Texas

Last week, I enjoyed tacos, tamales, and tejas music, learned more about how beautiful nature can be and the kindness of strangers. In between I developed a better appreciation for the diversity of our unique American experience, the great history we share, and how enriching it can be to meet new people.

When I look back to last week's business trip to Corpus Christi, I am astonished at how meaningful a few days out-of-town can be. Located in South Texas on the Gulf of Mexico, Corpus Christi has art, history, and science museums, celebrates music, just opened a new airport, and enjoys a lavish heritage.

The community has 277,000 people who care about one another. The front pages of the *Corpus Christi Caller Times* featured articles on the need to help the homeless, find minority participants for the National Marrow Donor Center, and it promoted community pride by featuring kids who have contributed hundreds of hours to community service helping those less fortunate.

One day of outdoor work brought me sunburn, it felt good. I jogged morning and evening back and forth along the two miles of downtown waterfront that featured sailboat marinas, palm trees and blooming hibiscus in beautiful grassy parks, stilt-legged cranes, a good breeze, and one morning I saw a red fox.

Mornings were best. One glance at the orange sun peeking over the horizon and I was hooked to stop and stare at God's use of light and color in transforming sky, water and land from darkness to light. It was the perfect way of signaling hope for a new day.

Corpus Christi is near the King Ranch, an 825,000-acre enterprise with 60,000 cattle, citrus groves, cowboys, 300 horses, black dirt, live oak and mesquite trees, and the rest you can imagine. It was founded in 1853 by Captain Richard King, a riverboat captain.

Padre Island is also nearby. Padre is the largest barrier island (133,000 acres, 110 miles long) in America.

The Spanish treasure fleet also made it one of the richest areas in the world. The island and its surrounding waters are known as a ship grave yard for all the old treasure ships that were sunk hundreds of years ago in bad weather. Christian programming and Tex-Mex music dominate the radio dial, but a little space was saved for National Public Radio and the classics.

Selena Quintanilla Perez, known simply as Selena, was a native of Corpus Christi. She is honored there today with a memorial and life-sized bronze statute recognizing her as a positive role model for youth. At the time of her death in 1995, Selena was 22-years old and the nation's brightest star in the Tejano music sky.

On the flight back from Texas, my seatmate was Debra Skriba, a native of Dallas who was traveling to Washington on business. The encounter with Debra, a Ph.D in humanities, is an example of the richness that strangers bring when they break down barriers of shyness. It was an extraordinary time to learn more about her experiences teaching at University of Chicago and Stanford, and management consulting with nonprofit organizations in the Dallas area. She had traveled the world, met fabulous people, read amazing books, and was artful and energetic in conversation.

I also had the opportunity to meet Renee Goodson, a traveling emissary for The Susan G. Komen Breast Cancer Foundation. Renee is articulate, smart, and devoted to the Komen mission of eradicating breast cancer as a life threatening disease. It was great fun learning that we both know many of the same inspiring personalities. For the uninitiated, Komen is headquartered in Dallas with 130 staff members who coordinate the efforts of 75,000 volunteers. Importantly, they invest millions in donated dollars for meaningful research to battle the terrible toll that breast cancer is taking in America.

It's hard to imagine a little business trip of better value. I can only hope that my employer feels the same way!

The National Marrow Donor Program

More minorities are needed for entrance into the National Marrow Donor Registry. Marrow donation is a relatively simple, easy process that saves lives of those suffering from various forms of cancer.

We often read about leukemia patients: kids, teenagers, and adults who need a marrow transplant as their last best hope for survival. When that happens, relatives are tested to determine the compatibility of their marrow. About 30 percent of these tests are compatible; however, when they are not a search is made among the four million registrants in the Marrow Donor Program. If that fails, special drives are conducted to find an individual who is compatible.

A few years ago, a couple in McLean, Virginia, spent over a million dollars testing volunteers for compatibility to save the life of their 18-year old son. None was found; the boy died.

Through a recent article in the *Corpus Christi Caller Times* I was reminded of the need for us, especially minorities to pull together to save lives in the National Marrow Donor Program. Entrance into the program requires a simple blood test. The US Department of Defense routinely does these tests for free; there are also special circumstances in the civilian community when the tests are free; otherwise, the cost is about $75.

Once entered into the program, a person remains there as a potential donor until age 60. It goes without saying that saving the life of another is everyone's highest and best calling.

The Importance of Saying *Yes*

There is a woman living in Alexandria, Virginia, who says yes to almost everything. Through an experiment in living she found that she's happier that way.

But there was a time when she was a miserable naysayer who just wanted to be by herself. She came to be positive by first hitting bottom with a horrible state of attitudinal health. One day Lynn Drake realized that she was disgusted with her life. Like everyone, she was a born winner, but also like many others she had let herself become a loser.

She was in a rut where the biggest thing in her day was rushing home from work to drink wine and watch television. Lynn had the TV schedule memorized, and it was through the television that she came to realize how low her ratings were with herself and everyone else. She had allowed her social contacts to languish, she didn't have a boyfriend, there wasn't any passion in her life, no direction, there were morning hangovers, and she didn't feel good about herself.

Her creativity, confidence and self-esteem were down and she had almost lost touch with her core being.

There is something wonderful about people who get depressed, hit bottom, and find the ingenuity, discipline and energy to re-ignite their inner flame. Lynn looked in the mirror, didn't like the reflection, and vowed to change.

She made up rules that would guide her back to the road of recovery. First, she would go out several nights a week whether she wanted to or not, she knew it would be an effort in planning and cost money, but she remembered her love of people and social settings.

Second, she would take one trip a month to learn about people and events in other places.

Third, she'd take an adult learning or college class every three months on subjects that interested her. She might learn a foreign language, learn how to quilt, or study geology.

Fourth, every time she'd find herself next to someone she didn't know, she'd strike up a conversation.

Fifth, she vowed to say **yes** to every opportunity.

Sixth, she would try to find her spiritual being through religious attendance.

Seventh, she would involve herself in fitness activities, try yoga, maybe walk-run, and swim.

A few weeks after starting her life anew with this powerful combination of rules a true test occurred. It was a rainy Friday evening and had been a long work week. Just before walking out of her office, the phone rang, it was her girlfriend Sharon. She wanted to know if Lynn could stop by happy hour on the way home to meet a guy named Bill and several others. Lynn didn't want to go, she was tired, but remembering that **yes** was her watchword, she reluctantly agreed. It was a pivotal decision; Bill became first her boyfriend, later her husband.

Besides Bill, other good things happened in her life. She found new friends, strangers that she met at airports, train stations, restaurants, and church. One person was a professor of anthropology. The professor stimulated her interest in the antiquities of Egypt, a country she grew to love. While hiking in Virginia's Blueridge Mountains she met an author who encouraged her to pursue a dormant talent in creative writing. Then there was the cowboy in Denver, he stimulated her interest in horseback riding, a passion she pursues today.

At church she loved the optimistic spirit of her fellow parishioners, the stained glass, and music. She also discovered that she had a deep passion to help others. Lynn's life changed, her spirit became one of optimism, humility, and curiosity.

Those around her were drawn to her charisma, her job prospects changed dramatically as she took a series of increasingly responsible positions in marketing. When they moved into their new home, Bill and his friends carried in his television. In arranging the living room, he asked where she thought it should go. Lynn looked at it, looked at Bill, thought a moment and told him to put it in a closet or the basement until they could give it away. He raised his eyebrows slightly, smiled, and gave a slight nod.

Best of all, she never forgot that her success started with a few simple rules, foremost in her mind was saying *yes* to every opportunity. Lynn is now breathing deeply of personal liberation and she smiles a lot. She is a little of you, a little of me, and a little of the guy or gal down the street. All of us reach points that necessitate change; we can ignore the signs or embrace the process. Lynn Drake is a model for courageously changing to make life better for herself and everyone around her.

The Small Fry Department

Recent observations from the Small Fry Department: Last week, gerbils Shadow and Lucky died. Their funeral was held November 6 in a backyard at Monroe, Michigan. My grandniece, Ashley Nichols, 7, orchestrated final rites for her pets by inviting every kid in the neighborhood. Each child said a few words as the little bodies were laid to rest. Ashley gave the final tribute for lives well lived, *they were the best gerbils I ever had.*

Closer to home, on November 4 at Hutchison Elementary School, Herndon, Virginia, my 10-year old daughter, Mary Virginia, stepped out-of-line by kicking three other girls. Although she was placed in detention by the principal for her use of excessive force, I wasn't necessarily displeased with her behavior.

Since they were in kindergarten together, Mary and Jesse Curling, a 12-year old with Down's syndrome, have been best friends. In this case, the three girls were tormenting Jesse. Mary's indiscreet use of force was excessive, decisive and overwhelming, but her heart was on the right beat. Helping, protecting and defending should be part of everyone's mission regardless of age.

Thanksgiving in America

This is our formal season of Thanksgiving in America. Everyday millions of people have their life changed. There are gains and losses, but no one stays in place for long.

Babies are born; people fall in love; a few win the lottery; others get a job promotion; positive, life-altering ideas are learned from books, movies and conversation; some will learn or be reminded about how wonderful the people in their lives can be; and many fortunate people will find out that their cancer is in remission. Hats are thrown in the air; people cheer and cry with happiness as families and friends celebrate. That's Thanksgiving.

To balance life's credits with a few debits, people are being killed—sometimes accidentally, often with purposeful design; there is abuse of defenseless children and the elderly; there is a new rank being added to America's army of the hungry and homeless; thousands of people are finding out for the first time that they are contracted a life-threatening disease; others are unconsciously allowing envy, fear, greed, hate, or vengeance to gain control of their lives while some of us are simply getting depressed over any one of a hundred things that can pull us down.

There are conversations in which loved ones needlessly shout obscenities at one another; and drivers are exchanging one finger salutes over absolutely nothing except vanity. We chat, lie and steal from one another and ourselves, sometimes without a second thought. When the going gets tough, when we're in a rut, the spirit of gratitude is difficult to muster.

Human beings are brilliant, all of us are. But we're also complicated creatures who create expectations, norms, and mores of behavior that confound us. The hustle and bustle of our emotions and the tempo of life cause us to forget about God's benevolence, we lose touch with ourselves without even realizing it.

Last week, my former coworker, Lieutenant Paul Norris, a two-time survivor of cancer (brain and lung) was killed in a one car automobile accident near Raleigh, North Carolina. Although Paul had retired and moved away from the Washington area 10-years earlier, his wife Linda called within hours to tell us about the tragedy. Everyone liked Paul; he oozed street smarts, survived life with good humor and optimism, and gave something of himself to everyone around him.

A few days later, coworker Carlos Alers was working in Panama when he suffered chest pains. After being rushed to the nearest hospital, examining physicians determined he needed immediate triple by-pass surgery for his survival from heart disease. Once on the operating table, they actually did a quadruple by-pass. Carlos is now resting well in recovery with family near.

I also learned that a nice woman in Colorado was diagnosed with metastasized cancer to her lungs, liver and maybe the brain. Physically fit and endowed with a positive attitude, her initial diagnosis of breast cancer was done just three months ago. At that time, she had a lumpectomy. None of these events was fair, but they happened.

We can believe that tragic, sad events dominate the world. If you want that to be your reality, so be it.

However, Thanksgivings should happen on a daily basis even when things aren't good. Adopting an attitude of gratitude for the broad range of blessings in our lives is the start of a personal liberation that insulates us against life's setbacks.

Several years ago, I found myself alone for Thanksgiving. It wasn't a happy time, but I made it significantly more meaningful and positive by writing out a list of all the things I had to be thankful for. Then I made a second list of all the things I could do to be more thankful in the future. Both lists extended into the hundreds of items. I've been busy ever since correcting past mistakes and creating more value by giving to others.

From that small exercise I learned that once our minds are oriented in a positive direction, we become truly fruitful in creativity, energy, productivity, and, yes, gratitude. Although we would soon tire of eating turkey, dressing, and cranberry sauce every day, a sense of daily Thanksgiving marks us as a celebrant of life at its best.

Historical Illiteracy

We are becoming a nation historically illiterate. That's sad. It means we're losing touch with our roots, the touchstones of our society, and the sacrifices of past generations. Young adults today have significant problems understanding historical events, and the major personalities heroic to America.

I just finished reading a 32-year old book that sets the stage for events to follow in our country. It's about fairly ordinary people faced with extraordinary circumstances. They rose to the challenge, but not without terrible losses. I hope you will read it and encourage a young person to do the same.

A Little Commonwealth by John Demos was written in 1970, that it is still in print is testimonial to the fine quality of this volume. A book right for the times, it recounts family life in the Plymouth Colony. Founded in 1620 by religious separatists and adventurers, the initial group of 102 Pilgrims came to what would become America in 1620 on board the *Mayflower*. Fifty-four of them survived the first winter; the second ship arrived in 1621, which was the *Fortune*. My ancestor, Edouard Bompasse (anglicized to Bumpus), a French Huguenot and an indentured servant, was among the 34 passengers on *Fortune*.

In America today there are 25 million descendants of the *Mayflower* contingent, and about 20,000 descendants of Edouard Bompasse (Bumpus).

I loved this book because it described a heritage of European customs and lifestyles that belong to the rooting of America. The book discusses housing, farming, Indians, raising kids, marital relationships, caring for the elderly, neighborly caring and support, church attendance, clothing, material possession, and death.

There is hardship beyond belief; great community leaders evolved which kept the growing Plymouth Colony stable as it expanded to encompass many small towns in Southern Massachusetts. A few of the noteworthy personalities among these first settlers were William Bradford, Myles Standish, Priscilla Mullens, and John Alden.

A professor of history at Yale University, Dr. Demos draws heavily on demographics and the behavioral sciences of anthropology, sociology, and psychology to help us better understand these first immigrants who sought our shores for religious freedom. It you like learning about America's heritage and I hope you do, *A Little Commonwealth* is a book right for you.

Moving to Singapore

My grandmother, Murl Mae Bumpus Welch, remembered for her calm, serene nature, has never let me forget my youthful wanderlust. Although she passed away 11 years ago, the switching's she gave me for disobediently running off again and again are still with me.

As a restless spirit of 4-5 years old, I drove her to fits. Mercifully, I moved with dad, mother, and my sister Linda to a rural setting in Michigan. It was about 20-miles from grandma's house and that seemed to suit us both fine. There I roamed field and forest, waded streams and through deep snow drifts, explored old barns, climbed huge trees, and breathed the freshness of natural discovery.

My dad didn't believe in striking a child, and mom just let me roam, so my curiosity for the world got fulfilled as fast as my little legs to could carry me. As a teenager I rode a bike over unexplored paths, learned to hitchhike, and loved driving old jalopies over little-traveled country roads. At age 17, I joined the US Navy seeing for the first time oceans, mountains, palm trees, water buffalo, rice paddies, typhoons, volcanoes, and big cities. I learned about poor, mostly happy people; saw dirty, smelly ports; made my first travel by airplane and learned to love living aboard ship.

The people I met were from everywhere in America and many foreign countries. Through my travels with the Navy I learned for the first time that color, religion, and material well-being separated people, some outright hating one another. Just as it affects you, I was and continue to be uncomfortable seeing widespread disharmony.

Now residing in Virginia for 18 years, I've decided to re-live the adventurous nature of my youth rather than grow old in satisfaction over a life mostly well lived. In a few weeks I am off to Singapore for a 3-5 year assignment with my agency, the Naval

Criminal Investigative Service. It's not easy packing your bags and flying off 10,000 miles on faith that life will be greatly changed for the better, but that's what will happen.

According to Charles *Tremendous* Jones of Mechanicsburg, Pennsylvania, I have nothing to worry about. Charles is an author and speaker who spent a lifetime traveling, thinking and writing. In his view, we only experience personal growth three ways: through the books that we read, people we meet and the places we visit. There are no sure bets in life, but Charles' opinion on the human condition is probably close to the mark.

Singapore is one of earth's garden spots. A small island three times the size of Washington, DC, there are four million people living there. The per capita income is the 18th highest in the world; the island is extraordinarily clean and the crime rate extremely low. Dealing drugs in an automatic death penalty, chewing gum is frowned upon, and jaywalking is a no-no. Remember the caning incident several years ago? A teenage American boy was caught spray painting cars. He was sentenced to several strokes of the cane, which caused an international furor for the tough sentence. Some said the boy got what he deserved.

It's also the lightning strike capital of the world, has beautiful beaches, and a colorful British colonial history.

There is a monsoon season and the annual rainfall is 120 inches, almost 4 times what we receive in Virginia. Vegetation is lush, orchids and bromeliads are abundant, and there is a rain forest.

English is one of four official languages; about 70 percent of the population is Chinese, 15 percent Indian, and 10 percent Malaysian. The remaining hundred thousands are people like me, expatriates from any of a hundred different countries.

Singapore officially celebrates religious holidays for Muslims, Buddhists, Hindus, and Christians; and there are 20 Presbyterian churches conducting separate services in Chinese and English. Toastmasters International has 114 Clubs in Singapore, Josephine Lee is my Toastmasters sponsor, and she'll be helping me get with the best group for my personality.

To counter the congestion, the island has one of the most modern airports, metro rail and bus systems in the world. Their society is unique because Asian cultures are blended harmoniously. People like and respect one another and the government officially promotes courtesy. This allows everyone to learn and be enriched by the presence of those who are different. I love that!

Singapore is a financial capital and significant for manufacturing computer and communications equipment. It's also a mecca for shopping and rest and relaxation. Coffee shops and cafes are abundant; many are along the Singapore River. And that's where I want to be to think and watch the water pass while sipping morning, midday or evening coffee. Let the adventure begin!

La Maddellena

Ciao! That's my greeting to let you know I've crossed seven time zones to spend two weeks on business in Italy. Then, of course, I flew back through those same time zones to get myself into the zombie state-of-mind just time for Halloween.

For those who have never visited Italy, don't delay as you're depriving yourself of a wonderful adventure at one of earth's most endearing garden spots.

Italy has 58 million friendly people, 98 percent literacy, and almost everyone believes in God. The people are superstitious, industrious, friendly, and promote art, music, and family values. At the time of my visit, McDonald's wasn't making much headway there. Italians love slow food, which they celebrate with festivals devoted to chocolate, pasta, gelato (ice cream), cheese, and wine. Good things to eat are at every street corner restaurant and café. Sometimes the water is bad and in those places people often drink good wine. Actually, they drink wine, lots of it, even when the water is good.

The Italians love art, which is on a colorful parade in their paintings, music, poetry, architecture, theater and dance. Life on the boot-shaped Italian peninsula is thousands of year's old, antiquity is reflected in Roman ruins and newer structures that have a classically ornate appearance with surrounding piazzas and fountains.

The Camorra (mafia) got its start and thrives in Italy, especially in the south on the island of Sicily. Although there are about two million people unemployed, neither homelessness nor public drunkenness are issues.

Italy is a melting pot of culture with strong influences from Germany, France, Slovenia, and Greece. Everyone speaks the melodic Italian language with accompanying hand and arm gestures, sometimes they also speak English.

My first week was spent at La Maddellena, a small island off the coast of Sardinia. With just 16,000 people living mostly in the island's one small town, this is a place to enjoy a quiet setting with simple people in an exquisite natural setting. Most of the island is a national park with flora comparable to Northern California. There are beautiful large granite outcroppings, high rugged hills with goats, and clear waters that reflect orange-red sunsets.

Besides discovering the wonder of pizze al pescatora (pizza with seafood) and riso alla pescatora (rice with seafood), the most remarkable experience was running along the coast road enjoying the wind, panoramic seascapes, and a touching display of starlight. Because of the island's isolation from light pollution, it's possible to experience heavenly sights not normally seen by city slickers. I now have a new appreciation for the night sky and all that is there that I can't usually see.

In the small world department, a hundred and twenty years ago, La Maddellena provided granite used for foundation stones on America's Statue of Liberty. Whether in the timeless strength of its rocks or its people, Italy possesses richness in the human fiber that should be the envy of the world.

World of Glad Tidings

Last week, Dan and Darby Jo Arakelian became parents to daughter Brenna Anne. Weighing in at 5 lb, 13 oz; Brenna's dad reports she is *...very healthy and super-cute.* Dan and Darby left many friends in Virginia when they relocated to Rochester Hills, Michigan in September. In reflecting on this newborn I am reminded that baby's are miracle beings and most especially for new parents.

Have you noticed that kids and dogs seem to be having the happiest times? Recently, Christine Cawayan of Alexandria, Virginia, treated her miniature dachshund, Barton, to a first birthday party with his neighborhood doggy friends. The K-9 troop dined on a bone shaped cake made of peanut butter and other good things.

My grandnephew, David, 10, likes goats. He and other fourth graders at Trinity Lutheran Elementary in Monroe, Michigan, got their moms to make cookies for a bake sale so they could raise money for a goat. They scraped together $126 which was enough buy and ship their new goat to a needy family in Africa.

In Charlo, Montana, Bobbie Culp celebrated Thanksgiving in a big way. She had just learned that her third bout of cancer in 20 years was in remission. It is scarcely possible to find a happier human being.

I am thankful for teachers, not only those who get our brains up and running, but those who kindly share their culinary skills. Anne O'Hara allowed me to be part of her family on Thanksgiving Day. I enjoyed kids, grandkids, her husband Jim, the in-laws, and the finest quality feast.

Besides her passion for cooking, Anne loves teaching fifth graders at Springhill Elementary in McLean, Virginia.

A few days later, I had the opportunity to be with Anna Tjoumas and her husband Angelo for another splendid meal. This one featured pastitso (Greek lasagna), Greek salad, Greek green beans, and brownies. My guess is that Anna is unexcelled in the preparation of Greek cuisine. She teaches special education kids in kindergarten and fifth grade at George C. Round Elementary in Manassas, Virginia.

If Romanian or Spanish is your native language, you will soon be able to obtain Peter Colwell's book, *Spell Success in Your Life* in new translations. Prefer English? Then get this wonderful motivational volume at amazon.com for about $15. First time author Peter Colwell resides with wife Trevia-Lynne at Germantown, Maryland.

Binjai and the Big Walk

Recently it was my privilege to smile my way through a visit to Brunei, a small country on the island of Borneo. Borneo is the world's third largest island and politically divided between Malaysia, Indonesia, and Brunei. That is probably more than you wanted or needed to know about this extraordinary part of the world.

What is more important is that Brunei has 350,000 great people, mostly Muslim. They are gregarious, honest, happy and particularly proud of their nation and the royal family. It is a wealthy little country with riches solidly built on character, religion and oil.

The Sultan of Brunei is second only to America's Bill Gates as the wealthiest man in the world. But he is first in the hearts of his countryman, they adore him for the progress he has brought and the respect and understanding he shows. Included amongst the great people of Brunei are about 50 Americans and 20,000 other expatriates from many other countries, most particularly Asian nations.

Highlights are pretty public parks, rainforests, ornate mosques, fine little restaurants, several interesting museums, and a water village with homes built on stilts.

The water village houses 30,000 people on the Brunei River at Bandar, the capitol city. The village is said to be the largest such community in the world.

My morning runs were usually along the Brunei River with thick rainforest as a frequent companion. On one of the outings, I heard the sound of what I imagined to be a large animal. In younger years such sounds would conjure a hope that I could outrun whatever might give chase, but times change. Now, I pin my hopes of jungle survival on being bigger, smarter, stronger, braver, or a better climber than whatever might like to eat me.

On my most profitable morning run I saw neon pink hibiscus and the explosive colors of bougainvillea that reminded me of fireworks on the Fourth of July. Besides the flowers I chanced upon a dead snake, 14 lively gibbon monkeys playing in a cemetery, and saw my first red dragonfly. The cooing of mourning doves perfected the experience.

On May 27, *Binjai* was cut down at Tutong, a district 18 miles from Bandar. The 200-year old tree was believed by village elders to possess a spirit that was contributing to nearby automobile accidents. Before removing the tree, officials from the Religious Affairs Department recited a doa (prayer) to remove any spirits that might be around the area. The doa was recited again after the tree was cut down.

Although *Binjai* has passed on drivers shouldn't raise their hopes that area roads will be safer. My one small criticism of Brunei is the excessive speeds on city streets and the tendency of drivers to run red lights. Like many people in the world, Bruneians are routinely in a rush for the sake of being in a rush. Now *Binjai* is gone, there will be no one to blame for auto accidents.

Juliana Hamdan looked at me with pleading eyes and said, *please join me, it'll be easy and fun, you'll like it.* Juliana was passionately plugging the *Big Walk*, a Sheraton Hotel Society and Sports Club event. I seldom say no, even in times when I should be more cautious and besides Juliana didn't seem like the kind of person who would mislead anyone.

As she explained it, the *Big Walk* was sponsored by the Sheraton and open to employees, guests and residents of Bandar.

Walkers were given a choice of a 45 or 55-minute trek through the adjoining rainforest. Everyone would start and finish in the parking lot, refreshments and door prizes were on the agenda.

Okay, this sounded doable and fun. There were 80-walkers. At the sound of the pre-recorded cannon blast we started up a trail, within 5 minutes my chest was heaving from the exertion of the continuing climb. From that point, the rigors of climbing and descending steeply profiled forest trails would be etched in my memory for a long time to come. Downhill paths were steps cut into hillsides with jungle vines, small wildflowers, ferns, bamboo, and canopy trees defining the neighborhood. I took the 55-minute trek, that's the one that had a hillside so steep that knotted ropes were used to pull myself up.

I felt woefully unconditioned, but was inspired by the children and elderly who were navigating the route with what appeared relative ease. At least they were smiling. Not everyone on the "Big Walk" looked happy. Juliana had also recruited them with the theme, ...*it will be easy and fun, you'll like it.* In fact, I saw Juliana sitting beside the trail, she was pooped, her engaging smile barely discernible. I asked how many times she'd been over this trail. She said it was her first.

Although I was an early finisher, probably somewhere in mid-pack, it took me 60-minutes. Like everyone else, I was soaked in sweat and covered in dust, yet happy with the encouraging applause that I received and then passed on to those finishing after me. Juliana was close to being right. Although it wasn't easy, memories often make hard things out to be fun. I remember being several thousand feet atop a ridge that overlooked the jungle and city of Bandar. That panoramic view was freely given to anyone willing to work at getting there. It was fun and I was glad to have been on the *Big Walk*.

From kids to the elderly, the Muslim people of Brunei were welcoming in speech and gesture, they are particularly adept at smiling, the most important part of an international language of affection, respect and understanding. I am grateful for the experience that brought me into contact with good people, educated me about spirit trees, and involved me in an activity that was *easy and fun.*

Remarkable People

The time in Michigan's Winter Wonderland was high quality. Some of the personalities that crossed my path were Sandy Sheldon, G. Carl Tonneburger, Arbie Thalacker, and Danyelle Campbell. They all have something in common that I'd like to tell you about.

Sandy Sheldon lives on the outskirts of Dundee, a little town in Southeastern Michigan. In 1978, she started walking for a problem with high blood pressure. The doctor wisely thought that she could better gain control of her health through exercise vs. medication. Twenty-five years later, she has traveled more than the circumference of the earth. That is over 24,889 miles a step at a time in a successful quest for good health. Sandy is one person in an army of national and international walkers who give us a sterling example of discipline and fitness.

Mr. Tonneburger celebrated his 100th Christmas in December. His brother married my great aunt Doris which means we're not closely related. Two years ago, Mr. Tonneburger was living in Florida and not doing too well so his daughter, Bonnie Nauts, took him into her home in Ann Arbor. On such skimpy information you probably can't read between the lines, but this is a love story between a daughter and dad with both being affected by TLC, one giving-the other receiving. We don't see enough of that in care for the elderly, when we do it is remarkable with its genesis in love.

When I am visiting Michigan, my dad, Larry Welch, Sr., and I like to listen to our cousin Jack Tonneburger play the organ at the Congregational Church at Britton. Over refreshments following one of the services, Reverend Dave Welcome, told me about his father-in-law, Arbie Thalacker, who had a mishap with his old Underwood typewriter. Mr. Thalacker could have taken the easy way and found another Underwood typewriter, but he didn't. At 96, he is doing well in diligently learning to use a computer.

If you ever wondered what can happen when you give a pony to a 10-year old, look no further than Danyelle Campbell. In December, Danyelle finished 11th in barrel racing at the National Finals Rodeo in Las Vegas. Her take for the year was over $80,000. She also trains horses and teaches kids how to ride from the family ranch at Washington, Utah. Danyelle is 26. She is my daughter's cousin on her mother's side; I am not much related to her either.

Lastly, I mention a fabulous trio who devoted themselves to The Salvation Army Red Kettle Program in Monroe, Michigan. My little nieces and nephew more than doubled normal Salvation Army contributions at the local Target Store. While Ashley, age 9, sang, *All I Want for Christmas is my Two Front Teeth*, Erin, 5; and David, 11, gave out candy canes and wished passersby a Merry Christmas. Yes, you guessed it; Ashley was missing her two front teeth and presented the irresistible lisping that is a favorite in that old Christmas song.

Everyone I mentioned, young and old, men and women, have commonality in that they are being their best. Excepting the kids who are capitalizing on their charisma, the adults are persisting in what we human's can do very well, live a good life. And they aren't even a drop in the bucket to all the personalities with positive attitudes who are transforming darkness to light. We all know our share of people who distinguish themselves in small and big ways; our challenge now is to learn how to be more like them.

A Respectable Vagabond

We're all blessed with a unique set of circumstances. Generally, we live out our good days surrounded by imperfection in ourselves, those around us, and in the situations we encounter. All this requires patience with ourselves and others, courage to face up to reality, and the dogged determination to believe that tomorrow will be better than yesterday and today. In between we find ourselves caring, loving and extending ourselves for others.

I am excited about our remarkable journey and the circumstances that define and enrich us. For my part, I thank God for my abundance in a wonderful family, pleasant friends and the opportunity to be a respectable vagabond, traveling the world with a job that puts me with good people in interesting locales.

Last week, I was in what was known as Siam, now called Thailand, a country that stands out as a true garden spot and one of the few nations in the world that has never been colonized by foreigners. There is a highly respected king and queen, and a simple tropical culture famed for silk, Buddhist temples, elephants, rain forests, tin mines, white beaches, mountains, streams and waterfalls, woodcarvings, and spirit houses.

Most, but not all of the populace practices the national pastime of smiling, old people look young, and the young look like kids. People are trim and healthy; they eat lots of fruit, vegetables and fish. A major industry of Thailand is exporting natural and human beauty by promoting eco-tourism.

Millions of people, but not too many Americans, flock to Thailand to be close to the sun, green growing vegetation, fragrant flowers, clean air, and friendly, handsome people. They swim, shop, trek through rain forests, drink beer, water ski, laugh, and hold hands while watching pretty sunsets.

A few tourists, those who overindulge at the banquet of ill-conceived ideas, take a taste of bungee jumping. The Thai people are a little like Italians, not so much for the humming of their many motorbikes or this plentiful supply of pizzerias, but for their love of kids and family. With 60 million people, the majority religion is Buddhism, along with a few Muslims and Christians amidst other religions.

I was enthralled with Thailand and its people. As a book lover, I was especially touched by the government's program, *Let's Love Reading*. The Thais have a 94 percent literacy rate, but they don't read much. Part of the reason for that is an undersupply of books, bookstores, and libraries and an oversupply of television sets. One of the recent books selected for publication in Thai is my friend Peter Colwell's book, *Spell Success in Your Life*, first published in the United States last year.

I spent six days at Phuket, an island resort 528 miles north of Singapore. Besides work, I jogged along Patong Beach mornings and evenings, went swimming every day, and generally absorbed the community spirit. One highlight was an elephant trek through a nearby rain forest. For moral support and good company, I was accompanied by Wanvisa Techo, her 7-year old son, Nice; and 8-year old niece, Tanoi.

We rode elephants, took a canoe ride, and saw monkeys doing more antics than I would have thought they were capable. I learned that monkeys can be trained to pick 400-500 coconuts a day. When Benjamin Franklin said, Idle hands are the devil's workshop, he wasn't referring to monkeys, but just like kids and we adults, they can be devilish when there is time to sit around twiddling their thumbs.

During a demonstration of elephant mental and physical agility, our trek guide asked for two volunteers, Wanvisa raised her hand and volunteered me as a prop. The baby elephants needed two humans to terrorize as they showed how bright they were bouncing one leg on our backs without squashing us. I knew it was all in good fun as I heard the audience's laughter. It's interesting how you think you're getting along pretty well with someone and then they volunteer you to be at the merciful play of elephants.

In the new friend's department, I had the distinction of crossing paths with Alan and Michelle Stoops and their daughter Annabelle. The Stoops were touring Thailand from their home in Liverpool, England. I felt especially close to Michelle as her husband had volunteered her as the other prop in the elephant show. As I said, we're all blessed with a unique set of circumstances with imperfections here and there, we meet good people in interesting locales, and that makes all the differ.

Andy Rooney

Last October I had the privilege of working at La Maddellena, Italy. Yes, I know, life is tough! On the third as a friendly conversation, I mentioned that when I day, one of my coworkers asked if anyone had ever told me that I reminded them of someone else...maybe someone famous.

Without much thought into what was asked, I answered that when I was young my nieces called me "Uncle Burt" after Burt Reynolds. When my questioner and others in the room stopped laughing, she commented that she had someone else in mind, Andy Rooney.

All I knew about Mr. Rooney was that he was old, a bit cranky, and presented interesting viewpoints on CBS's *60 Minutes*. I also asked myself, how in just 20-years could I regress from being Burt Reynolds to Andy Rooney? It was a social ambush of my own making.

A day earlier as my workmates from Washington discussed where we'd dine that evening, I told them I wasn't going to work all day and then spend half the evening with them, too. It wasn't a mean-spirited comment, but a reflection of my priorities, it's more important for me to use my free time reading, running, and relaxing. Although I was free of malice, unfortunately that's not the way it was interpreted. Now I was grumpy old Andy Rooney.

While back in Michigan for the holidays in December it was providence that I channel-surfed into an interview being conducted with Mr. Rooney by NBC's Tim Russert. I was spellbound. There I was on television, with all my crankiness and more. It was fun learning that Mr. Rooney has wry humor, is honest enough to admit mistakes, and at other times stubbornly sticks to his guns. I can imagine that he wouldn't go out with his workmates either, especially if there was a good book to read or a nap to be taken.

Although I hadn't felt any anguish for sticking by my right to privacy, I was validated by Mr. Rooney. After all, what can people expect from a cranky humorist who likes to read, run and rest? The purpose of Russert's interview was discussion of a new book that he had written, *Common Nonsense.* In talking about the book, I learned that Mr. Rooney had written many other books and that they were popular reading, if not occasionally controversial.

Common Nonsense was the first book I purchased at Singapore's Border's Books. I read it and now have to agree, I am like Andy Rooney. That's not bad and certainly not all good, but there comes a moment in everyone's life when they should face up to the truth. When we'd rather read, run, and relax than dine out with coworkers, we might as well admit it.

Street Life in Singapore

Singapore's street life is bustling. People walk briskly with purpose; they have energy and a sense of direction.

On Saturday mornings, kids, mostly young girls in their school uniforms, are out with little canisters collecting donations for a variety of charities. Of course, I like that, everyone does. When you drop a coin into the canister you get a smile of thanks and a sticker that identifies you as a good boy or girl, then others of these pre-teen solicitors won't bother you for donations later in the day.

When I jog early in the morning, I see a few men sleeping on cardboard underneath bridges. Cardboard is a universal material for the homeless, they find many good uses for it. The few that are awake make good humor, surprisingly common among homeless people around the world. They aren't supposed to sleep under bridges or be homeless. If the police catch them they go to social services for a home and a job, those two go hand-in-hand in Singapore. There aren't any free lunches, everyone carries their own load.

I pass stores that say Gucci, Armani, Starbucks, 7-Eleven and McDonalds. Two weeks ago, I was walking to the train station and a monkey ran across the street, climbed a tree and sneered at me. Why a monkey would choose to sneer at me is puzzling. I like bananas and generally credit my existence to having ancestors who climbed trees, walked mostly on all fours, and looked a lot like monkeys. Cousin, why did you sneer at me?

Several days later I walked out of Isetan, a 4-story department store with a supermarket in the basement. I had two bags of groceries. Outside the store, I walked past a marble park bench occupied by a young Singaporean woman. She smiled. I smiled and nodded, I thought I'd met her but for the life of me I couldn't remember the name. Curious, I looked back, she was walking toward me. We smiled again and although I didn't know her from Adam I gambled, shifting my groceries, I extended my hand and said, *It's nice to see you again!* As she smiled and took my hand, she gave me the secret handshake. The one that says, *Hey, wake up fool, I'm a streetwalker.* She confirmed the secret handshake with the question - *You want me to come with you?* Although I could have used help carrying the groceries I graciously declined.

Yesterday, I was walking to the metro station to catch a train to work. This was early in the morning and there weren't many people on the street. As I patiently waited at a pedestrian crossing, a young woman came up beside me and introduced herself as Amy. She told that she'd fallen on hard times and would be grateful if I'd *loan* her $50. Certainly this got my attention, even in Washington, DC, the best panhandlers are satisfied with a $1. Giving the situation a quick study, I decided to split the difference and gave her $4 for originality and good humor. She reluctantly thanked me before asking that I reconsider the $50. I should have asked for a donor sticker to exempt myself from the second solicitation.

Jaywalking is against the law in Singapore as is the sale of chewing gum, and spitting. I jaywalk, not every day, just sometimes. Other people do to. Something else that people do in Singapore is sit at sidewalk cafes like Starbucks and watch other people stroll past. They also do that in Italy, Greece, America, France, Germany, England and many other countries.

I love to make unique discoveries, and particularly enjoy the reassurance that monkey shines and people antics are such a wonderful part of life wherever you are.

A Person in China Sneezes

In all of recorded history there has never been a time when humanity wasn't confronted with war, natural disaster, disease or attack by one predator or another. There has always been something to challenge survival: we face it in our global village and in our personal lives. Scarcely anything is what it appears to be; our imaginations distort reality and create outsized emotions such as fear.

Take the two-striped telamonia spider, for example. Six weeks ago, I received an e-mail from a trek guide in Malaysia letting me know that a doctor in Singapore had identified bites by the two-striped telamonia spider as the agent of death for several people who had either dined in a certain Singapore restaurant or flown on Air India.

Medical investigators traced the course of the poisonous bites to nests of these spiders that were living beneath toilet seats. It's always something! I was so fascinated by the details I did some research: The two-striped telamonia spider, also known as the jumping spider, is native to Asia alright, but is not listed as being poisonous. I was encouraged.

Within minutes the Internet steered me to the web site *Urban Legends.* It seems that the spider story first surfaced in Chicago in 1999, it came up again in Jacksonville in 2002, now with a few minor changes in the details it was Singapore's turn to participate in the hoax. That's one of the threats we can laugh off as good-natured fun.

Another threat, this one serious, has been the source of your e-mails asking if I am safe from the severe acute respiratory syndrome (SARS) epidemic. The answer is yes, of course, I am fine and plan to continue that way. My biggest threat in Singapore is being hit on the head by a falling coconut while jogging. But SARS is serious business, there's no getting around it. It also illustrates how the world is shrinking. A person in China sneezes, another citizen in the global village is infected with a life-threatening ailment.

Medical researchers in Singapore and other locations have been doing a superhuman job in identifying the cause of SARS; more is being learned every day. One of the things to realize is that it won't be going away. The best we'll be able to do is isolate its properties and treat it with the right protocol. Most researchers believe it is a virus that jumped species from animals to humans. Other diseases that have done that are smallpox, HIV/AIDS, and mad cow disease.

Singapore has had 172 cases, and 16 deaths. Our local outbreak started in February by three women who had been exposed to the virus in Hong Kong. Esther Moke, a former flight attendant, deserves our prayers. As one of three SARS carriers from Hong Kong she infected 20 other people including 10 family members and 8 health care workers. At last count, her father and mother, and minister had passed away. She and her uncle are in critical care.

Our schools in Singapore were closed for several weeks. Now the kids are back to the classroom, teachers monitor them for fevers and each childcare center and school has an isolation room to put those with a fever; there are about 350 people who have been infected but are not ill; and are quarantined to their homes where they're monitored by electronic cameras and wrist bands.

The government makes home delivery of groceries; Singapore Airlines business is down 38 percent from a year ago; and the thoughtful, generous people of Singapore have created a Courage Fund to honor health care workers. Occasionally, I see someone wearing a surgical mask in public, but that is rare. Our major airport, Changi International, is doing a great job of screening incoming passengers, there are nurses meeting all flights and an electronic scanner (Infrared Fever Sensing System) alerts when anyone passing has a higher than normal body temperature.

There are 23,000 taxi drivers in Singapore; many are now voluntarily having their temperature taken daily to obtain a one-day fever free certificate that reassures passengers that they do not have the first symptom of SARS. Ridership in taxis is down 45-75 percent. Hotel occupancy has dropped from 70 percent to 20-30 percent; and the Singaporean economy has lost an estimated $900 million.

The newspapers, radio and television have done excellent work in educating the public. A recent Gallup poll disclosed that virtually every citizen was knowledgeable on the nature of the disease. The same poll showed that 75 percent of those responding were afraid that they or someone in their family would be exposed to the SARS virus.

The global village is smaller than we think, we may not need to watch our butts for poisonous spiders, but those sneezes and falling coconuts are another matter. It's always something!

Virginia, Montana, and Michigan

There are 50 superlative locations in the United States that make particularly good places to visit. I had the privilege this month to be at three of them: Virginia, Montana, and Michigan.

The trip to America had its genesis in a conference and training at Virginia Beach; thanks to my employer, the Naval Criminal Investigative Service, I was able to extend an additional week to be with my family in the West and Midwest.

Trekking 9,770 miles though 12 time zones in 24-hours is not for the faint of heart. The long flight is the reason more American's aren't swarming all over Asia. During my several weeks in the United States, I was overjoyed and overwhelmed with experiences that centered on being with good people in positive settings.

Because of my Toastmasters background, at the conclusion of our conference at Virginia Beach I was asked to present a traveling trophy to our best speaker. Without hesitation, my choice was Dr. Ray Morgan, one of my colleagues from Naples, Italy. Ray is educated and experienced as a forensic psychologist; he is also a superior speaker and human being who is authentic, confident and creditable. In watching Ray speak, I was reminded of the importance of presenting ourselves with the good grace that we all possess, but don't always use.

Thanks to Di Keith Jones, I was invited to be a volunteer at Richmond's Race for the Cure, an event to create awareness for the importance of early detection for breast cancer and to raise research funds. Although high wind, heavy rain and a sky streaked with lightning delayed start of the race for over an hour, the day was perfect. The Richmond community could have said the heck with it and went home soggy and disgusted, but didn't. Runners, walkers and volunteers stayed, kept their good spirits, and distinguished themselves as a group of special people.

Kellogg's, Ford, New Balance, Yoplait, Zeta Tau Alpha, and American Airlines continued their prominence as generous national sponsors, and Di finished the 5K (3.1 mile) event first in the survivor category with a time of 23:55. She is a huge inspiration to all who know her.

Over 5,000 people registered, they raised $250,000 to benefit breast cancer programs. Americans, just like every other nationality in the global village, are best when reaching out to help one another.

Saving the most interesting experience in Virginia for last, I had a pre-birthday lunch with daughter Mary. She will be 11 in June and is such a fabulous personality I couldn't help writing a book about her. Many of you have already read, *Mary Virginia, A Father's Story.* After I told her stories about rain forests, monkeys, elephants, water buffalo, and spirit houses in Asia, she is looking forward to Far East adventures in her own right

Flying from Virginia to Montana, I met Ralph Stockstad, a resident of Charlo, Montana. Ralph told me that Montana was second only to Alaska for scenic wilderness. Of course, Ralph is right. From Missoula, my daughter Christina's home, you can see snow-capped mountains, rivers, canyons, and valleys that are home to beaver, coyotes, black bear, moose, elk, antelope, mountain lions, and big horn sheep.

Not long ago, one of the residents of nearby Rattlesnake Valley had a problem getting to work. He couldn't get his front door open because a black bear had fallen asleep on his porch. Welcome to the West!

There are thousands of miles of trails for jogging and hiking. The Clark Fork River runs 360 miles through the area, it is fed by the nearby Blackfoot River, Bitterroot River, and Rattlesnake Creek.

This is Big Sky Country, home to Flathead Indians, Lewis and Clark's explorations, and the University of Montana. There are 57,000 people in Missoula; it is the state's second largest city. There isn't any commuter traffic and residents support themselves through service industries, farming and ranching. In my several days in Montana, I jogged for hours along the pristine and swiftly moving Clark Ford River, watched Christina and her friends play

ity of Helena.

Watching Christina play softball would make any father proud. She is a good sport, a supportive team player, and has fabulous hand-eye coordination ideally suited to sports like basketball, softball, and tennis. Although Helena has fewer than 24,000 residents, over 4,000 people registered their support for Montana's Race for the Cure fun run and 5K (3.1 miles) foot face. Their participation also signaled a desire to end breast cancer as a lift threatening disease. The Race for the Cure Series is presented by The Susan G. Komen Breast Cancer Foundation, the largest private funder of breast cancer research in America.

It was in Michigan that I first realized I most liked communities where church steeples are the highest structures in town. That happens in little towns throughout the Midwest and other parts of America, too. Michigan is where I grew up and where my family and oldest friends still live.

During several days there I spent time with my grandnephew David Nichols, 9, and his sisters Ashley Anne, 7, and Erin, 3. I also met Jan Sapchatana, a Thai expatriate at lunch with my dad and classmate Marcia Bolog.

My peanut gallery relatives are living extraordinary lives. Ashley was recently featured at the Monroe County Young Authors Conference for her book, *My Poem Book*, a richly illustrated collection of her poetry. Ash is also among a trio of neighborhood girls, all 7 and 8 year olds, who have their own cable television show, *Kids Talk Back*. She is a trained camera girl, while Samantha Shiflet and Chloe Kinsey perform as announcers.

Her sister Erin is also creative. In early May, she and Sam Kinsey, 3, played barbershop, now she has a short summer hairdo that was touched up by the local beautician and Sam's mother makes him wear a baseball cap to shield the world from Erin's handiwork.

David is a scholar, good citizen, and patriot. He has compassion, speaks up for individual rights, and has an international view of the world. Thanks to David and his teacher, John Boldt, I was invited to speak to the 4th grade class at Trinity Lutheran Elementary. I also spoke at Ashley's 2nd grade class with the kind permission of her teacher, Barbara AuBuchon. My topic for both presentations was, *Kids and Culture in Asia*. The highest and best contribution that we make in our lifetimes is mentoring children so I took this opportunity as an unusually high honor.

Lastly, Thai Jan Sapchatana works with my classmate, Marcia. Because of my recent travels to Thailand, we thought it would be a good idea to meet for lunch. Jan represents what has always been good about America—attracting pilgrims who arrive loaded with energy, ingenuity, and an extreme willingness to serve. People from all over the world come to the United States for safety and security, they generally bring with them more than they take away or use up. Jan is that kind of immigrant. She possesses a master's degree in finance and it's my guess that she has the integrity we desperately need in corporate accounting and finance.

Spring in Virginia, Montana and Michigan is an exquisite experience with fragrance of lilacs, lavender, and honeysuckle; pastel shaded tulips and irises, and the dainty pink, purple and white blossoms of redbud, cherry and apple trees. Jogging on country roads and backwoods' trails, the wildflowers whisper, *Look at us; look at us, aren't we pretty?* If the colors could be sound, they would be a soothing symphony lulling us to a love of life and the natural world in which we live. Of the 50 superlative locations in America, they all have the explosion of scenic beauty in common. Just like countries around the world, the United States is a treasury of nature that can leave us hearing the soft, gentle voice of the outdoors that says, *...aren't we pretty.* The world sure is!

Global Conflict

We're now making world history faster than most of us can comprehend meaning. Today, every American community is affected with the fear of losing loved ones to war in Iraq or terrorism; just before that we were worried about corporate greed, our economy, and the prospects for job security.

Caught in the middle, Iraqis are fearful that they won't survive the conflict. Before that, their biggest concerns were getting enough to eat, access to health care, and freedom of choice.

Six months ago, the war of misinformation and manipulation started creating tensions between global friends and partners. We ridiculed those who didn't share our enthusiasm for violent conflict; they said we were one-way, a bad reputation to have in the global village, and if that weren't enough we're accused of being vengeful and greedy for oil. We called them crapheads and cowards. Most obvious in the turn-of-event is that America has developed as a nation that can dazzle with star wars technology, yet disappoint in applying diplomacy to a world starving for peace.

Diplomacy requires lots of skill, it isn't just patience, but also involves understanding, respect, effective listening, and sacrifice. Everyone has to give something up, but everyone wins.

The conflict in Iraq is traumatizing about 11 million kids under age 18; and millions of people around the world are either protesting or expressing frustration with our limitations in nurturing global harmony. None of us can know the future; however, I'll stick my neck out and predict that besides bringing the fresh air of liberation to a well-deserving Iraqi people, a new American protocol will develop in better relating with our international friends and neighbors, whether they are African, Asian, European, Arabic or Hispanic. The difficult lessons of today will be tomorrow's human progress, that's how history works, it teaches us to be better people. I can't wait!

Mass Murder in Paradise

Last week I was working at Denpasar, Bali. That is the same Bali celebrated in movies and books as being a romantic paradise. People walk hand-in-hand along pretty beaches, trek through rain forests, and swim in clear blue ocean waters.

On October 12, 2002, the image changed from paradise to the scene of mass murder. In all, there were 509 victims from 18 countries, 200 died. Australia was especially hurt by the two terrorist attacks that left 88 of their young people dead. One bomb carried by a suicide bomber was detonated at the entrance to Paddy's Irish Pub while the second, a car bomb especially constructed to create extreme heat, exploded across the street in front of the Sari Club.

Those closest to the blast were incinerated, survivors suffered severe burns and cuts from millions of glass shards. The terrorists were radical Islamic extremists. They targeted entertainment centers, which were densely populated by young men and women on vacation. Evil thinker Osama bin Laden had fingered Australia because of its kinship to the United States and Australia's compassionate aid to the East Timorese in their bid for independence from Indonesia. East Timor is 98 percent Catholic, Indonesia is predominately Islamic.

Ironically, Bali is an island in the Indonesian chain, but is a Hindu community. A paradise is lost and the world is made more complicated by those on the lunatic fringe. It's easy to cry in unison over the obscenity in losing these young lives; much harder to stand shoulder-to-shoulder in solidarity to face the evil spirit of leaders like Osama bin Laden and Iraqi's shadowy president Saddam Hussein.

Peacekeeping at East Timor

Everyone should visit East Timor, the world's newest country. The circumstances aren't pretty, but the education is worth a million dollars in learning how the other half lives. In 1999, the 800,000 people in East Timor voted in a referendum for independence from Indonesia, 75 percent voted for liberation. If you wonder why they wanted independence consider that it's estimated that the Indonesians had killed 200,000 Timorese in the preceding 20 years.

At the time of voting, gangs collectively referred to as the Christian Militia struck by burning 70 percent of the buildings and murdering over a thousand people. One was a Dutch journalist, Sander Thoenes, 30. Although Indonesia denied involvement, circumstances suggested otherwise. The United Nations (UN) sent in 10,000 peacekeepers from 20 countries. They provided the Timorese breathing room and have helped reconstruct schools, churches, clinics, bridges, and public buildings.

Before the civil uprising the people of East Timor were poor, they're worse now. There are two ATMs in the country, no traffic signals, roads are in shambles and the beautiful natural beauty is covered with trash and shells of burnt buildings. Goats, pigs, dogs, and chickens run loose. Street lights either don't work or aren't turned on. City streets are black at night. It's hot and dusty, there are lots of orphans, and other kids are given up because parents don't have the resources to keep the family together. Because of her love for children, Inasiadas Flores Faria started an orphanage in her home that subsists on donations. She is now raising 16 kids; her own 5 children are grown.

Unemployment stands at 70 percent, some people grow coffee, and others are fishermen or work at small roadside stands selling seashells, bananas, lemons, coconuts, and bottled water. Some live in cottages with thatched roofs, those people better off have rusty corrugated metal roofs. Some homes have running water, others use community wells.

I learned two things in East Timor. The first is that poverty and happiness are compatible. The people I met were amazingly positive, friendly and cheerful. They kept their heads up! Secondly, soldiers with the United Nations, and civilians with the US Peace Corps, are powerful in their compassion and professionalism. They genuinely care. Currently, the   UN Humanitarian Mission for Peacekeeping is down to 3,700 troops with the largest teams coming from Japan, Singapore, Australia, South Korea, Malaysia, Thailand, Portugal, Pakistan, and Nepal. The Peace Corps has 50 volunteers living with host families.

Next time the US or our foreign assistance is criticized; stop, think, and remember the gifts of faith and hope brought to millions of destitute people just like those in East Timor. The US is as relevant as the concept of compassion.

Underwear Robbers of Singapore

Singapore is a city, island and country. It doesn't snow here, there's no ice, and I don't think the temperature ever drops below 75 degrees. I am among 14,000 expatriate Americans who work mostly for multinational corporations or the US government.

The culture is different from anywhere else in the world. Singaporeans are ethnically related to the Chinese, Malayans, and Indians. They practice their religions in mosques, temples, churches, and synagogues. Although different, they mix well, enjoy one another, and are more respectful of humanity than most people in the world.

This is an interesting place for many reasons, but today I'd like to just tackle monkeys, brassieres and underpants.

Vivian Tang is a stock broker who relieves the stress of her life by training for and running marathons. One of Vivian's problems is the monkeys that populate Singapore's Upper Pierce Reservoir. Seems as though people tend to feed the little beggars and they expect every passerby to give them a handout. On a recent run, Vivian found herself surrounded by these panhandlers and all she had to offer was a scream. Monkeys being pretty smart got the message.

Singapore also has the underwear robbers who occasionally enter well-to-do homes and make off with cash, jewelry, and expensive electronic goods. There are three of them and they wear T-shirts with their underpants. In keeping with the spirit of robbing people while attired in their underwear, they tie up their victims with brassieres (I am not making this up!).

Brassieres also reflect the humanitarian spirit of Singaporean women. Not long ago a TV station sponsored an event to challenge the Guinness Book of Records on the 30,000 bras that had been tied together by residents in Boston, Massachusetts. Singaporeans, women and their male supporters, tied together 80,000 bras for breast cancer and raised $30,000 in the process. As I mentioned, Singapore is an interesting place.

Wild Malaysia

For the past several weeks I've had the privilege of business travel through Malaysia. If we could have made the trip together, I am convinced that you would have been as impressed as I was with the natural beauty and friendliness of the people.

For the geographically challenged, Malaysia's capital, Kuala Lumpur, is 184 miles north of Singapore. The country has 22 million people, most are Muslims, and ethnically they are Malay, Chinese, Indians and Original People. I saw some important things and now won't be the same in my global perspective.

Not many Americans visit Malaysia, but millions of people from other locales do. They come to this wonderful country to climb caves and mountains, watch birds, fish, swim, sun themselves and enjoy the abundant natural beauty.

Phoebe Chan is a wilderness guide working out of Kota Kinabalu. She says people like to trek through the rainforest and live in tents. In the forest, Phoebe's groups share the space with leopards, tigers, Sun Bear, lizards, snakes, wild boar (nasty tempered pigs) and lots of monkeys. Three-fourths of Malaysia is jungle, the Original People (Native Malaysians) have strong spiritual ties to the wilderness just as our Native Americans have with their natural heritage.

As I understand it, some of the Original People, especially on Borneo, were headhunters and cannibals. Time, custom and tastes have changed; Phoebe says they don't do that anymore.

The official language is Bahasa Melayu, but Malaysians speak any of 15 other languages, almost everyone is fluent in English. They have a high literacy rate (83 percent) and a strong economy with a smaller percentage below the poverty line (8 percent) than in the USA. They earn and spend ringgits; most of their national income is derived from tin mining, petroleum, electronics, logging, palm oil, rubber trees and tourism.

Besides Kuala Lumpur, I visited Panang, Kota Kinabalu, Langkawi, Kuantan, and Lumut. On one early morning jog at Langkawi, I saw seven monkeys, three flying lemurs, a Monitor Lizard (road kill), a stampeding herd of cattle running on the road, many egrets and low flying bats, assorted tropical birds, four beautiful Tom Turkeys, and a peach-shaded horizon as the sun rose from a turquoise-colored sea.

I also heard early morning prayers emanating from countryside mosques. The most enjoyable part of the jog was to meet so many friendly people who waved, smiled, and spoke from their cars, motor scooters, and roadside stands. There were Muslims, they didn't hate me, a Christian; to my knowledge they simply saw another human being doing something interesting that they wanted to acknowledge.

On another morning, this one at Lumut, I sat eating breakfast near the hotel's swimming pool. There were three Muslims at the pool—a father, mother and their 2-year old son. As they played in shallow water with the boy, I saw classic family affection and a tenderness that speaks the universal language of love. We may have different religions, nationalities, economic circumstances, and educations, but when it comes to love, we're all the same, especially with our children.

While I was enjoying my work in Malaysia, the world continued to spin and people did interesting things. At Ouyen, Australia, 5 women took their clothes off at a secret location as part of a ritual rain dance to bring relief to farmland in the state of Victoria. A week earlier they had practiced and it sprinkled.

Sadly, in Japan 1,200 people, mostly middle-aged men, committed suicide. Japan has the highest suicide rate in the developed world, about 30,000 a year. Psychologists believe it's because of their 12-year economic recession. I don't think there are any good reasons to take a human life, most especially anything having to do with money.

The people in Argentina also care about money. Because of their economic collapse, they are stealing the country blind for anything metallic to scrap in making ends meet for their families. Statues, manhole covers, traffic lights, copper telephone wires, and electric meters are all disappearing.

There are many paths to heaven, a retired banker in Beijing, China, has found one of them. The gentleman heard about a 500-year old turtle that had been caught by fishermen in the South China Sea. Just before it was turned into soup, this Good Samaritan put up the equivalent of $90 to see that the ancient mariner was returned to the sea.

Saving the best for last, while in Malaysia, I met Cathy Tate, wife of America's Naval Attaché in Kuala Lumpur, Captain Bob Tate. Cathy is an inspiration in representing the United States. A registered nurse, she volunteers two days a week at Hospice for Malaysia. Cathy told me that the best way to free your life from negative distractions is to devote yourself as a helpmate to others. Good advice!

Wherever you have spent the past several weeks, I hope you were also inspired, hopeful for the human condition, and enjoyed the awesome beauty of our world.

Singapore's Sister Teresa

Her well-groomed silver hair framed an angelic face of smooth, unblemished skin. Alert brown eyes shined as her smile extended to laughter. She started our time together by telling everyone about a long-tailed monkey that talked too much, the main character in a parable of her own making.

Following the story, which was a reflective account of her popularity and after our own laugher had faded, her tone shifted to quiet resolve as she explained her life's mission to benefit the poor and needy. The only thing missing was her halo.

Teresa Hsu is a role model for compassion and humanitarian values. She explains one of her values as being core to all that follow: "There's no religion but the religion of love." Better known as Sister Teresa, she is 105-years old and still travels the world promoting kindness, peace and understanding. Before our meeting, all I knew about Teresa was her age, that she had never worn glasses, and that she was a devotee of yoga.

On a recent Sunday morning, I had the opportunity to meet Sister Teresa at her modest home in a suburb of Singapore. My good fortune was the result of kind friends, Nisa Wichitsiri and Rebecca Phay, who guided me to this remarkable woman. Positive people have a way of finding one another even if the path twists and turns over time and distance. That was the situation I felt as we sat is Teresa's reception room.

Born in 1898 in Guangdong province in Southern China, she has had a remarkable life shaped by unique circumstances. An abused child, Teresa and her three brothers and sisters were physically and verbally abused by a violent father. Probably because of that experience none ever married and Teresa and her siblings following a way of enlightenment that included teaching, nursing, the priesthood, and helping others wherever they could.

In 1925, she was able to enroll in a work-study program that allowed her a sufficient education to qualify as a secretary. When the Japanese invaded China, she quit her job to become a volunteer caring for the casualties of war. At the war's end, she went to England for a nursing education and work; then came an eight-year stint with the German charity group Bruderhof in Paraguay.

Finding her way to Singapore in 1963, she started the Heart-to-Heart Service while a matron of the Kwong Wait Shin Hospital. Two years later, she chartered the Home for the Aged Sick at Jalan Payoh Lai in Singapore.

In 1983, at age 85 and under bitter protest, she was asked to step aside at the nursing home started by her and her sister, Ursula. She had been relieved because of age, not incompetence, and it made her angry and distrustful of government rules.

Today, Sister Teresa's Heart-to-Heart Service continues strong as she and other volunteers provide basic food stuffs and money to 14 elderly people and 4 families who are struggling to maintain a home. Heart-to-Heart functions efficiently on a shoestring budget from her modest home. When asked to describe her priorities, she said, she wears second-hand clothes as it is too difficult to buy new things when she knows there are hungry people doing without life's basic needs.

Last year, Sister Teresa was honored in Taiwan with presentation of the Love for Life Award by the Chow Ta Kwan Education and Cultural Foundation. When she met Taiwan's President Chen Shui Bian she took a gentle jab at the president's yoga techniques. She is also the recipient of the Guinness Stout Effort Award and the Singapore Life Insurance Association Award for her charity work.

In the past year, she has been featured on talk radio in Singapore to discuss techniques in caring for the elderly, been a yoga instructor and peace activist in Australia and is currently arranging trips to Cambodia and Vietnam to promote care of the aged.

Listening to Sister Teresa's straight talk leaves no doubt as to what's on her mind. She is direct and plain spoken in her truth. Her words of wisdom are as vigorous and fresh as spring blossoms:

No happy person expresses themselves in a hurtful way. This is my understanding of human nature.

You are as young and happy as you want to be.

I know there is no greater teacher than Jesus Christ. He was tortured, hanged on a cross and all he had to say was 'forgive them, for they know not what they do.' What greater love can there be?

There is only one Teresa Hsu; she is more unique, kinder, and compassionate than you or me. All of us are a light unto the darkness, but her light is brighter, her flame

ignites the inner spirit, it illuminates and spreads faith and hope showing people how grace is defined.

I wish you could have spent that Sunday morning with Sister Teresa, just as I did, you would also have become an improved person in the process.

Three Weeks in India

After three weeks in India, I am able to add a few more pieces to the puzzle that makes up our world. We're wearing different clothes; believe in different religions; some of us are poor, others rich. The world is complex, but most people are easy to understand. Everyone, no matter where they live or who they are have a basic need for nourishment of the heart, body and mind. People in India are all these things and, of course, more than I'll ever be able to express.

I like writing about good people and India is busting at the seams with the finest personalities that you'll find anywhere. During my travels I visited Kochi, Mumbai, Vasco da Gama, and Chennai. Not everything is pretty in the land of Mahatma Gandhi and Mother Teresa. There are rundown buildings and run down people.

In Mumbai (formerly Bombay), a community of 16 million, I saw thousands of homeless people living on sidewalks where they sleep, eat, brush their teeth, and play with their children. There were millions that I didn't see; Mumbai has the world's largest slum. The heavy traffic; often disorderly and chaotic, included buses, trucks, and small taxis. There were also bicycles, horses, and bullocks pulling carts and wagons with vegetables, building supplies and ice. There were cattle being driven along the streets by old women, packs of lazy dogs sleeping in the shade, and large gatherings of noisy crows.

The Victorian architecture of Mumbai is gorgeous, but not well maintained. The Prince of Wales Museum is educational in helping patrons understand India's rich culture, history, and religions. It's filled with kids in clean and neatly pressed school uniforms learning about their heritage. Other kids are playing cricket, the national sport; riding their bicycles, roller skating, and using skate boards.

While kids are at early morning play, their parents and grandparents walk, stretch and pray in the sunrise hours on the boardwalk and beach at Mumbai. When they pray, they think of the sun, earth, fire, air, water and the universe as having meaning in their lives. Beggars are in every nook and cranny; they are mostly satisfied to receive a few rupees for food. One morning I saw a young woman create a glorious chalk drawing of God on a sidewalk near my hotel. People dropped rupee coins on the creation in appreciation. The woman was poor; she looked malnourished, but possessed a magnificent artistic gift.

In another contrast, Mumbai is also the capital of India's Bollywood, a highly creative community of film makers. There are reputed to be more millionaires in Mumbai than in Manhattan. I know the Bollywooders are not sharing enough of their good fortune with their neighbors just as I know the global community is not doing enough to help the less fortunate in third world countries like India.

My taxi driver in Mumbai, Opie Mishra, told me he liked Americans best. I challenged him on the comment, but he backed it up by saying he liked Americans best because of goodwill visits to Mumbai by President Bill Clinton and actor Richard Gere. Clinton had a successful 5-day diplomatic trip to India in 2000 and Gere visits periodically in support of Gere Foundation India, which operates 25 health clinics to combat AIDS. Okay, Americans are the best, that's what Opie said.

Traveling south to the state of Goa, I visited the community of Vasco de Gama. While India was once a British colony, Goa was under control of Portugal. Thirty percent of the population there is Christian, sixty-five percent Hindu, and five percent Muslim. With 1.3 million people, it has the highest per capita income in India, about $660 annually. The literacy rate is also among the highest at 76 percent. Goa is cleaner, greener, and more westernized than Mumbai; over a million tourists visit annually. They are mostly from Europe and arrive by cruise ship and charter aircraft.

I jogged on narrow country roads that snaked through canopies of tall coconut palms. My vistas were rice paddies with snowy-white egrets strolling on long legs; small farms with pigs, chickens and cows; and the Arabian Sea was never far from sight. There were fresh ocean breezes that sometimes carried the scent of cow manure--for those who love animals, farming, and the outdoors, cow manure is not necessarily a bad smell, it's just part of the country landscape.

Joggers are a rarity, people stared, smiled and said hello. I stopped now and then to visit with farmers and vegetable peddlers, they liked me--not because I was an American so much as I was just like them--curious, friendly and respectful. On one of those country roads I came within 10-feet of being bonked on the head by a falling coconut. Wherever I traveled in Southern India, merchants liked to barter, so do I. Passing through the markets is enjoyable because sellers derive such joy in communicating, companionship with strangers, and the chance to make a sale. Although they would never think of stealing your wallet, they do not hesitate to coax buyers into purchasing overpriced merchandise. There were times when I paid more than things were worth, but it was not without respectful verbal sparring that left me smiling for having matched wits with very bright people.

In jogging one early morning at Kochi, I noticed the trucks; there were hundreds of them lined up waiting to receive cargo at the port. These were not ordinary trucks, they were works of art with cabs beautifully adorned with colorful paintings of tigers, elephants, sunrises, God and Jesus, birds, butterflies, flowers, and panoramic landscapes. Running beside the long line of trucks was comparable to strolling through an art gallery with wood and metal substituted for canvas.

Kochi was also where I noticed that women sweep the streets while men supervised. They also collect garbage, dig ditches and perform construction work under the same circumstances.

I asked Sunayana Shukla about the inequity, she was quick to respond that society hasn't always been fair to women in India, but life is changing quickly. She continued to explain that new opportunities were opening up every day for educated women to accept leadership roles in all areas of their society. Sunayana had just earned her master's degree in business administration and is a manager at the Taj Malabar Hotel. The world is a big place. There are moving parts and puzzle pieces in the human condition that we can't feel, touch, or smell from pictures. Visiting India is to develop a sense for the colorful diversity that makes the world bright, it also leads to a sense that there is brotherhood and sisterhood within the human family wherever we reside. We can also get a sense for the compassion and goodwill that is needed whether our neighbors are living on our street or halfway around the world.

Turning in their Graves

Last week, the earth gave a small rumble as some of my ancestors turned over in their grave. I hate it when that happens; it means I screwed up again. The day started innocently enough. At 4:25 am, I left home for a 90-minute jog on the streets of Singapore. Mornings are best, the air is cooler and cleaner, and there is more privacy from cars and people.

It was an enjoyable time zigging up one street, sagging in a new direction, going up and down hills, turning left, then right, heading north, south, east and west, no point of the compass was exempt.

The tropical birds were singing early morning songs, the stars bright, and an occasional frog hopped out of my path. At the time I should have noticed familiar landmarks on the turn journey home was the moment I realized my math skills were rusty, 2 plus 2 was not equaling 4.

Unfazed by what I should have recognized as a flawed sense of direction, I kept running north when the most direct route home was south. Finally, curiosity and fatigue got the best of me, I asked an elderly couple for directions. Almost everyone in Singapore speaks English, but not this couple.

I next asked a young man at a bus stop. He spoke English, but could only say he wasn't familiar with my street and I needed to take the train home. Hailing a third stranger, I found someone who knew where I lived. He was gracious enough not to ask if I was truly from outer space, but did offer that I needed to take the train home. With no money for train fare, I exercised my usual flare for stubbornness and ran home.

The journey that started innocently enough was completed by 7:30 am, I was late for work, tired, embarrassed and disgusted. From time to time, we all arrive at the crossroads of decision where we must ask ourselves for honest answers to important questions. The decision I had to make was will I go to work or go swimming?

The choice was clear. With hand to sweaty forehead I conjured a low grade fever and could feel a tickle that signaled the approach of a sore throat. I made the fateful call. Because of the SARS epidemic, my workmates were fearful, not so much for me, but they thought I'd already infected them.

The ancestor's rumble was loud enough that they may have turned over twice while thinking, *Who would have ever thought we'd contribute to such a lack of direction and creative storytelling in one puny descendent.*

US-Vietnamese Relationship

The Vietnamese have several favorite Americans. One is John McCain, another is Hillary Clinton. As a former prisoner of war, Senator McCain has been an unlikely champion of the Vietnamese people; and Senator Clinton is well-remembered from a historic 2000 visit she made with the president and daughter Chelsea. Angelina Jolie is thought of as an angel for her goodwill toward Asia and support of Cambodian orphans. Brendan Frazer and Britain's Sir Michael Caine are famous for their 2002 filming of *The Quiet American* outside Old Saigon's Opera House on Lam Son Square. Other Americans most just like me with no particular claim to fame, are greeted by the Vietnamese people as minor celebrities.

Last week I had the opportunity to visit Ho Chi Minh City (formerly Saigon), meet people and watch, listen and learn. It was an exquisite experience in an exotic part of the world. Although the USA's entrepreneurial spirit was not allowed a return to Vietnam until nine years ago, the landscape now has some, but not too many reminders of American culture. The kindly Colonel Sanders is there with his finger-lickin' good chicken, people snack high calories with Swenson's Ice Cream, my favorite soft drink Pepsi leads Coca-Cola in popularity, signs advertise Mobil and Kodak; Citibank occupies a large, opulent building, and Sheraton and Marriott make guests feel welcome. There is a Ford dealership, but Honda motorbikes are the vehicle of choice. Dell is a popular choice among computer users and Motorola dominates in communications.

Ho Chi Minh City is no small fry. There are 8 million people who move themselves around by bicycle and motorbike. The streets start humming with motorbikes at 5 am. At that time people are gathering in pretty parks to stretch, play badminton and volleyball, and do Tai Chi; this happens while venders are preparing breakfast at curbside for busy people.

The sounds, sights and smells give an aura of high energy and excitement. By 6 am, the sunrise is bathing pastel-shaded French colonial buildings in visually pleasing warmth; and bright-eyed kids in clean, neatly pressed uniforms have joined the movement toward their schools and colleges. The smart-looking girls wear white pant-skirt-blouse sets called ao dai, the boys are well-dressed in blue pants and white shirts, and some wear blue ties. Their parents and older brothers and sisters are headed off to work in westernized clothing, some in baseball caps that say NY Yankees, and there are Nike shoes.

I ran morning and evening along these busy streets. Pedestrians and bikers could not have been more friendly or encouraging, especially when I wore my t-shirt with the American flag. Kids waved, little girls blew kisses, men gave me two thumbs up, and others just stared as people sometimes do at strangers. All in all, I felt like a gold medalist!

There are 8,000 Americans living in Vietnam. They are a collection of former boat people returned to their homeland, some are businessmen and women, there are war veterans and government employees, and hundreds of inspired volunteers benefiting humanitarian projects. There is a brotherhood and sisterhood in the USA-Vietnamese relationship. In the past 20 years, the Vietnamese have been the largest single nationality migrating to the United States. Vietnamese women have married American men, and as was explained to me several times, Vietnamese women really like American men. Thanks to Hollywood and our good behavior, we have a favorable reputation. A story about one good man came to me from 28-year old Tran Thi Mong Chinh, a retailer at C&C Zakka Fashion on Dong Khoi Street. Chinh told me that she grew up with the most adorable boy, his name was Hy and he was Amerasian. Ten years ago, his American father returned to Old Saigon, married his mother and took them both back to the United States. Hy is now a medical student at George Washington University.

Vietnam is a communist country of 81 million people, red flags with a yellow star fly above government buildings in Ho Chi Minh City. As in many countries there is a difference between north and south. South Vietnam differs from the north in language nuances, but more importantly the income levels in the south are significantly higher. Ho Chi Minh City contributes 43 percent of Vietnam's gross national product; enterprise is more fluid in the south and that attracts higher energy, innovation and a creativity that is propelling the nation to a brighter future. America is Vietnam's biggest export partner; Singapore is its biggest import partner.

Emi Yamauchi is the US Consulate General at Ho Chi Minh City and on September 11 I was one of a dozen of her dinner guests. It was through her patriotism that we were brought together to remember the 9/11 tragedy in a moment of solemn reflection on those who died, their families and the angelic rescue crew. Emi is a role model for diplomacy of the United States. As a Foreign Service Officer, she is one of the thousands of careerists who serve, often in difficult circumstances, to maintain our relationships with people in distant lands. Everywhere we travel outside the United States there are several things you can count on: The State Department will have a professional cadre of savvy personalities representing America, and the Peace Corps will be serving with distinction. You can also expect that you'll be treated like a celebrity as long as you're willing to look up to others in the same spirit.

In 2003 we see a strengthening of the US and Vietnamese relationship, some of that is attributable to governments, but the highest quality is people-to-people, one day at a time, one person at a time. Isn't that the way we get to a better world?

Tonga on the Fourth of July

Floats and a festival make the Fourth of July special. Beauty queens waved from floats, kids ogled, men smiled and everyone tapped their toes to the sound of music. That's the way it was at Nuku-alofa, Tonga, on the Fourth of July.

There were American flags and US Sailors and Marines marching along with soldiers and sailors from France, New Zealand and Tonga. The US Peace Corps was there along with their counterparts from Japan, Australia, and New Zealand. But all the hoopla had little to do with America's Independence Day and everything to do with the King of Tonga. He was celebrating his 85th birthday.

There is a lot of affection in Tonga for the king, in fact, the capital city, Nuku-alofa, means abode of love. The Polynesian people are friendly, they like each other and strangers are treated like celebrities. They also love food. The king holds the record for being the world's heaviest monarch. In 1976, he weighed in at a hefty 444 pounds, now more slim and fit, he has trimmed down to a mere 300 pounds.

With 100,000 people living on fewer than 40 South Pacific islands, Tonga is far from a tourist haven. There aren't any fancy hotels. Most visitors stay in bed and breakfast accommodations, which provide the advantage of bringing outsiders into more intimate contact with Tongans. Besides the friendly people I met at two bed and breakfast inns, I chanced upon pigs, chickens, and dogs that run loose in a natural setting that wouldn't be complete without them. Take snorting pigs, crowing roosters and barking dogs combined with the laughter of children playing amongst palms, breadfruit trees and poinsettia shrubs, cover it all with a canopy of blue sky or twinkling stars, throw in a view of the Pacific

Ocean and there you have it, in one sentence, the scene I enjoyed at Tonga.

Jogging beside the ocean on Vuna Road in early morning darkness, I had two memorable experiences. One morning out of the shadows came a porker, neither of us expected to see the other. Porky was startled and snorted, I used my newly acquired adrenaline to jump, then ran in the other direction. Both of us survived, later I read that visitors were encouraged not to interact with the pigs because they are held in such high regard by their owners.

On another jog before sunrise I ran through a village that already had 5 small children playing beside the road. Seeing me they started laughing and giggled as they joined in the run. Jogging up the road, one little girl, the one with no shoes and a thick braid of black hair down her back, took my hand and we ran side-by-side. She chatted away in a mixture of English and Tongan, most of which I couldn't understand. She probably couldn't understand me either, but comprehending words was less important than being together as we all laughed along on our happy jaunt. Little girls don't often take my hand and share their stories, when it happens I count that as one of life's great moments.

George may also have good moments to remember. That's not his real first name for reasons that will become apparent; and I never knew his last name, he's just one of those characters you meet now and then traveling around. A white-haired elderly man from Australia, he was visiting Tonga to find a Polynesian woman to take care of him in his advancing years. It will clarify the theme here to know that George is part of that fellowship known as lecherous old goats. He wasn't planning to be at Tonga long so he was doubling his chances of meeting a willing *caregiver* by inviting young women to *interview for* the role two at a time. Although George's interpretation of senior citizen care differs from mine, I was pleased with the results: He didn't experience a heart attack; the young ladies earned some extra pa-angas (Tongan money) as George paid for their *interview* time, and not one of the prospects took him up on his offer.

Tonga is 6,000 miles from Singapore in the South Pacific. Mutiny on the Bounty took place off the coast in 1789. Captain Bligh and 18 of his men sought refuge on "Tonga, but barely escaped with their lives. The natives practiced cannibalism back in those days. Diets changed, now the population is virtually 100 percent Christian. Methodists and Mormons are the dominant religions, but many others are present. The churches are numerous and part of the missionary effort is represented in religious-sponsored schools and colleges.

On Sundays, stores are closed; it is a quiet time for families who attend two to three services at one or more of the numerous churches.

There is also a German community. Local lore says the Germans came to Tonga years ago to keep an eye on the British, liked what they found, and stayed on. If you're wondering about the Italians, they are represented by Angelo Crapanzano and his wife Mele. The Crapanzanos are owners of Little Italy Pizzeria, reputed to be the best pizzeria in the South Pacific. There are no McDonald's, KFC, or Burger King and that's best!

Tonga is a place filled with my kind of people: they love a parade, eat well, treat their pigs with respect, raised great kids, and take good care of the elderly when they deserve it. Sorry, George!

2 + 4 = 6

A month ago, while on travel I spent an overnight in New Zealand. That's where I met Niueni Perese Koteka. She was waitressing at The Galloping Duck, a nondescript restaurant not far from Auckland's international airport.

What made this encounter such a memorable occasion was the aura of joy that Niueni wore. She went about her duties with a facial expression that showed a grin waiting impatiently to broaden into a huge smile, her stride was shoulders-back pride, and she possessed the grace that touches we humans when things are extraordinarily good. In short, Niueni had an attitude glowing with optimism.

There was something going on and she wanted to share it. Knowing the answer, I asked if she was having a good day.

Niueni couldn't wait to let me know the details. It was her birthday and she was 30. From where I stand, having your 30th birthday is a good thing. I wished I could remember my 30th. But wait, there's more!

Niueni also wanted the world to know that the doctor had called her on her 30th birthday; she is going to be the mother of twins. The twins will be arriving around Christmastime to join their four brothers and sisters. Let's count that up, 4+2 = 6, 30-years old. My sense of charity thought of the father.

Niueni told me that Eddie was the best father and the best husband and that he was elated. I was glad to hear this news as I don't often hear wives brag about what wonderful fathers and husbands there are in the world. I am not sure where I will be at Christmas, that's a long way off, however; my mind will be on Niueni, Eddie and 4 + 2 = 6.

Sister Teresa Revisited

Two weeks ago, I had the privilege of again working with Singapore's Sister Teresa and many of her volunteers in giving food, financial aid, and a morale boost to elderly and needy families. A legend, Teresa Hsu is the 105-year old leader of the nonprofit organization, Heart-to-Heart Service, an effort that she chartered in 1963.

On what is usually the last Sunday of the month, she summons her volunteers to deliver rice, coffee, sugar, tea, cooking oil and other staples to those in need. Although there is no visible homelessness among Singapore's four million residents, there is an enormous need for supplemental assistance in public housing units.

In my September session with Heart-to-Heart nearly 40 men, women and children volunteered to make deliveries of foodstuffs and visit with recipients. It was also a special day as a local television crew was filming a segment on Teresa for the program *True Courage*. Following team camaraderie and assignment of those without transportation to those with their own vehicle, we loaded our groceries and headed out.

Irene Phua drove and a young Singaporean man, Kathi, accompanied us. We dropped our bags at the home of two elderly women who lived in a two-room flat. They were frail, but cheery. I could also see that they were grateful for the assistance, but I could only communicate by listening to Irene and the ladies talk in Chinese. I couldn't understand the words, but I could see grace on the face of Irene and the two elderly ladies.

Irene questioned the ladies about any needs they might have for special foods, medicines, or ointments. Earlier in the month, Sister Teresa had provided the ladies cash to help pay for their rent, doctor's bills, and the purchase of fresh food.

The charity of Heart-to-Heart in Singapore is not unique, there are many organizations staffed by thousands of volunteers who generously contribute materials, money and time to benefit the less fortunate.

Future generations will judge us on how well we cared for the disenfranchised and underserved people of the world. There won't be many who care about how rich our society was in a material sense, but how wealthy we were in spirit to extend ourselves for others. Sister Teresa and those like her are the real enlightened leaders of the world; all we have to do is follow their path.

A Maryland Fight Promoter

Two weeks ago, I called a friend who is a fight promoter in Maryland. I should call people more than I do, especially friends who get me motivated in the right direction. When our lives get crowded with one thing or another it's too easy to let time pass and not give the important people in our lives the attention they deserve.

That's what happened to Kim and me. Kim Henry started promoting her fight against breast cancer in 1992, she was 31 years old and it would be 6 years before she contracted her own bout with breast cancer. She promoted the fight through fund raising and voluntarism for The Susan G. Komen Breast Cancer Foundation, fed the homeless, and was a community leader in Toastmasters International.

Our paths crossed with pleasant frequency. On August 24, 1998, life changed for Kim. She was diagnosed with breast cancer and opted for a mastectomy; five weeks later she stood in front of a Toastmasters audience to make the case for improved breast cancer research and treatment. Kim was lucky; her cancer went into remission and stayed that way for two years. In 2000, the disease metastasized (spread), she resumed appointments with oncologists again sticking with regiments of medication, radiation and chemo therapy. It's been ups and downs, her life is threatened, she fights fear, feels pain, cries, loses ground and gains some back. As she slogs through the goop, Kim has never lost faith, hope and optimism. She also believes in the benevolence of God, prays, smiles, and lovingly reassures those around her. Those who know Kim are stirred by her example of humanity.

At about this time two years ago, she was magnificent in promoting the fight against breast cancer in front of three hundred of my coworkers at the Naval Criminal Investigative Service in Washington, DC.

The Federal Combined Campaign had just started its $200 million charity drive. Kim was there to recommend The Komen Foundation. She spoke of her experiences and those of other breast cancer patients; listeners were touched, many later contributed generously to breast cancer research. Our director, David Brant, led applause as he followed her at the lectern. Expressing his admiration for Kim, he wondered out loud how many of those present that day could stand and speak so eloquently about such an important topic. There was another round of applause as people recognized not just eloquence, but a young woman who stood for something bigger than herself—improved health care for women.

Two months ago, Kim was leaving her oncologist's office, took a misstep, fell and broke her leg. The femur was shattered to the point that doctors considered insertion of a pin to be the best option. That also required putting a pin into the good leg so that they would balance. She now lives at Silver Spring's Holy Cross Hospital and is undergoing physical therapy to regain the ability to walk; she is battling cancer and has a degenerative eye disease. As a testimonial to how positively she has affected her co-workers, they have continued to donate their vacation time so that she can keep drawing a regular paycheck. That's love for you!

If you'd like to make an important gesture, whether you know her or not, send Kim a note of encouragement. I guarantee that you'll feel good about it, and can you imagine how much your concern will mean to her? Her address is Kimberly Henry, Holy Cross Nursing Rehabilitation Center (Room 233B), 3415 Greencastle Road, Silver Spring, Maryland (telephone (301) 388-1563)

October is Breast Cancer Awareness Month, a right time to send a donation to The Susan G. Komen Breast Cancer Foundation. If you'd like to do that in honor of Kim, send a check to The Susan G. Komen Breast Cancer Foundation, 5005 LBJ Freeway, Suite 250, Dallas, Texas 75244. Put in a note indicating that the check is on behalf of Kim Henry and provide her address. Komen will let her know that you've made a donation in her name.

Dr. Albert Schweitzer

Fifty years ago this month, the 1952 Nobel Peace Prize was awarded to Dr. Albert Schweitzer. He wasn't there and the honor was accepted in his behalf by the French ambassador to Norway; however, Dr. Schweitzer knew what he would do with the $38,000 prize. It would be used toward the expenses of constructing a leprosy hospital in Gabon, a country in West Africa.

We don't hear much of Dr. Schweitzer anymore and that's a pity. His life was a model of high moral principle. He was enormously gifted, but his fame and the love of a grateful world came from his capacity to give of himself and encourage others to do the same. I like that.

Dr. Schweitzer was born in 1895 at Alsace, France; he died in 1965 at Lambarene, Gabon. He was 90. Between birth and death he attained an extraordinary education, wrote books, played music, and on his 30th birthday decided to devote the rest of his life to the natives of equatorial Africa as a doctor of medicine. When he told his family and friends of his decision, some were angry and other cried in disappointment because he had such enormous talent as a musician and preacher.

Dr. Schweitzer possessed 11 Ph.Ds. He studied for and was awarded doctorates in music, theology, philosophy, and medicine; seven were honorary degrees. As a musician, he was an expert on Bach and used his considerable musical talent at organ concerts in Europe to raise funds to build and maintain a medical infrastructure at Lambarene. A prolific writer, he wrote books on Bach, organ construction, religion, philosophy and his experiences. He was also a husband and father.

In 1913, he established a small hospital at Lambarene where during the day he delivered health care to what would ultimately become thousands upon thousands of natives. At night, he wrote scholarly books, which further financed his interest in providing medical care to Africans.

In all, Dr. Schweitzer made 14 sojourns to Africa. On each occasion he stayed several years before rotating back to Europe to recruit more volunteer doctors and nurses and raise funds to maintain and continue expansion of the hospital. When I reflect on Dr. Schweitzer's contributions to humanity, I think of the hundreds of thousands of people that are with us today because of the lifesaving talents that he generously gave to their ancestors.

In his youth, Dr. Schweitzer developed a philosophy to guide his life. He called it *Reverence for Live,* an ethic that incorporated love, kindliness, sympathy, and empathy in its deepest and highest sense for mankind. He practiced what he believed and in the process gave us a model to live by. We should think about Dr. Schweitzer's example, think about incorporating personal philosophies like *Reverence for Life.* We might not transform the health care of a country in Africa, but we'd make our little slice of the world pie the best it can be and that's not bad.

Thanksgiving in Vietnam

This is Thanksgiving week in the United States. The holiday has its origin in the Pilgrim's arrival in America; tradition suggests that the first Thanksgiving was celebrated out of gratitude for life and friendship with the Indians. Nearly 400 years later, we still feel what the Pilgrim's felt—gratitude for life and the blessings of good relationships.

Last week I was in Vietnam, a country generating goodwill, prosperity, and affection for all of us in the global village. Working with my employer, the U.S. Naval Criminal Investigative Service, I was privileged to witness the historic return of America's Navy to Saigon, which is one of the districts that comprise Ho Chi Minh City.

City parks were manicured to perfection, the streets immaculate; and as befits a great nation, communist or not, the people were warm and affectionate. The guided-missile frigate *USS Vandergrift* arrived in Saigon on November 19. Four days later they left their mooring for return to the ship's home waters in Japan.

In those four days, the crew of 200 mostly young men were interviewed by CNN and Associated Press reporters, drank cold beer; shopped, visited an orphanage and school for the disadvantaged, laid a floral wreath at the statue of Ho Chi Minh, hosted tours and receptions aboard their ship, and had a competitive volleyball match with Vietnamese sailors.

We can't underestimate the friendship value of 200 ambassadors of goodwill brought together from America's mix of culture, race, and religion. It was a classically fine reunion, the smiles of young men caused the hearts of young women to skip a beat; and an older generation remembered a war that is now fading from memory. That's Thanksgiving! We forget and forgive, and give thanks for what is good about today. I like that!

A Buddhist country of 80 million people, Vietnam is moving up in prestige, popularity, and purpose. The people are industrious, often working every day of the week; and kids get plenty of encouragement to stay focused on their studies.

While at Ho Chi Minh City, I noticed thousands of people congregating in city parks as early as 4:30 am to stretch, walk, jog, and play at the national sport of badminton. They are old, young, male and female. Their direction and energy was notable. The old tended to stretch together to the rhythm of music or the direction of a leader; daughters walked with their mothers, and the young moved faster and sweat more. I imagined that everyone was in a thankful frame of mind. Exercising people are like that; they are busy thinking positive thoughts. Men and women do not live by bread alone—those who exercise must eat and just so American expatriates don't forget it's a time for feasting, the Renaissance and other big hotels served delicious Thanksgiving Day buffets. As good as it was, the quality of their buffets may not be the equal of the Noodle Soup Restaurant in Saigon. They advertise *No Delicious, No Pay*. If that concept were more widely adopted, we'd have a little more to be thankful for.

Santa Claus is coming to Vietnam. Christmas decorations on major stores suggest that it's a good time to buy. There were artificial Christmas trees just like the real thing, bright lights were blinking, and make-believe reindeer pulled sleights.

Another holiday with plenty of merit is Teacher's Day, celebrated on November 20. That was the day when Vietnam's students thanked their teachers by showering them with cards, gifts and bouquets of flowers. As they should be, teachers in Vietnam are appreciated—the sale of flowers in Ho Chi Minh City jumped 60 percent.

Nanci Griffith passed through Vietnam last week. She was there to give a concert in Hanoi supporting the Vietnam Veterans of America Foundation. Nanci is a fine country-folk singer and songwriter from Texas. The Vietnam Veterans of America Foundation was founded in 1980 as a humanitarian organization helping people in Kosovo, Cambodia and Vietnam who suffered injuries caused by war or contracted diseases such as polio. This mission is to provide artificial limbs, braces and wheelchairs through their own clinics. They leave thankful people in their wake.

One day I rode a high-speed passenger ferry from Saigon to the seaside community of Vung Tau. While there I jogged on a beach beside the South China Sea, rested, watched people, and listened to their stories.

The best time was with a group of taxi drivers who had abandoned their taxis to play poker at a small plastic table on the sidewalk. They knew a smidgen of English, I wasn't as bright in their language. The communication barrier notwithstanding, we passed the time enjoyably each learning a little about the other.

Returning to Saigon on the ferry, a 2-year old girl and I brought delight to her parents and other passengers as I taught her one of my best skills—blowing kisses!

Thanksgiving is a good holiday, there's no doubt about it. It's especially rich when we adopt a theme of gratitude for all the good people in our international community. The strong are helping the weak, brothers are lifting sisters, the healthy are tending the sick, and kids are learning to blow kisses. I like what the Pilgrims started; all we have to do is keep the spirit alive!

V.P. Menon

Two weeks ago, I experienced another of life's great moments, this one at the Dhoby Ghaut metro station in Singapore. It was there that I learned something about people making a good connection.

The evening weather had been threatening, there was thunder and lightning, and sprinkles but now the rain was falling in buckets from a black nighttime sky.

As I entered the train station with umbrella in hand, a young woman looked at me and smiled. Strange women looking at me and smiling happens so rarely, I most often don't know how to respond.

In this case, I smiled in return and said hello, but didn't lose my stride in heading toward the escalator to meet my train home. Riding the moving steps, I wondered why she had done that. Within seconds, I knew the answer.

Reaching the bottom level, I took another escalator back up, walked up to the woman and said, *Do you want my umbrella?* She was speechless with surprise, but managed to blurt out that she'd been waiting for 30-minutes for the rain to stop.

I handed her the umbrella, and headed back to the escalator. She asked, *How can I return it?* I told her she couldn't, but she could pass it to a stranger who needs an umbrella.

Reaching my station at Orchard Road, I walked three blocks home in the rain. I was soaked, but happy a stranger had allowed the opportunity to make a classic connection: a person in need and a person willing to share. How was the woman affected? I'd say that she already knew the high value of a good smile at the right moment. More important she learned something about V.P Menon's spirit of giving.

Two days after the Great Umbrella Giveaway, I read a brief account of V.P. Menon. V.P. was one of the most significant political figures in India during its struggle for independence from Britain.

The eldest son of twelve children, he quit school at thirteen and worked as a laborer, coal miner, factory hand, merchant, and school teacher. He had no degree and no family ties to support his ambitions, but he grew to be one of the prominent people who made freedom possible for his country.

In his lifetime, he was known for cool efficiency and an ability to promote harmony between his people and the British. He also enjoyed a reputation for personal charity, a value he learned early in life under unusual circumstances.

As a young man newly arrived in Delhi to seek his first job in government, all his possessions, including money, were stolen. In desperation he turned to an elderly Sikh, described his plight, and asked for a loan of 15 rupees to tide him over. The Sikh gave him the money, but when V.P. asked for his address so that he might repay the loan, the Sikh said that he owed the debt to any stranger who came to him in need, as long as he lived. The help came from a stranger and was to be repaid to a stranger. He never forgot that debt, even on his death bed.

At that unfortunate time a beggar came to the family home in Bangalore asking for help to buy sandals as his feet were covered with sores, V.P. asked his daughter to take 15 rupees from his wallet and give it to the beggar. That was his last conscious act. I learned this story from Robert Fulghum's book, *All I Really Need to Know I Learned in Kindergarten*.

A smile, giving away an umbrella, helping a stranger, walking in the rain, reading a good book—we very often find the human spirit to be right where it should be.

Ceasefire in Sri Lanka

A warm morning sun and the sound of surf rolling on a pretty beach are two things that get me excited. Every day last week I was out to this sort of new beginning while jogging along Calle Road in downtown Colombo. Colombo is a community of 2.2 million people and is the political, financial and cultural capital of Sri Lanka. It's a place you leave knowing that your life has been made better by the experience. Thanks to the Awn family: Majid, Leena, Maleena, and Nabil, I learned more than most strangers do about a new land.

An island nation off the southern coast of India, Sri Lanka produces major-label clothing for the world, leads in the mining of gemstones, and is one our most productive tea growing countries. There are elephants, monkeys, and leopards. The people are faithful, most are Buddhist, others worship as Christians, Muslims and Hindus. Religion is a private matter; diversity is a high cultural value among the nation's 20-million people.

Sri Lanka has a perplexing population. They are among the world's best natured and pleasant people, so you may wonder why they have spent the past 20-years fighting a terrible civil war. Many Sri Lankans ask themselves the same question. A country of colonial distinction, it was once known as Ceylon and profited from the presence of the Portuguese, then the Dutch and finally the British who provided them independence in 1948.

Buildings have beautiful European architecture, streets are spotless, parks neatly tended, and fountains cascade pleasantly amidst tropical foliage. The streets are filled with a rainbow of tapestry as women stroll in their brightly colored cotton and silk saris. Kids are dressed in neat-as-a-pin school uniforms, traffic officers ride horses, and an occasional ox cart mixes in with small cars and buses.

It would be an idyllic setting except on most street corners there is likely to be several armed soldiers near a sandbagged bunker. There has been a good cease-fire for two years, but neither side lets down its guard until issues are resolved. During the civil war there were 66 suicide bombings, and in all the fighting over 60,000 people were killed.

Americans and Sri Lankans stand shoulder-to-shoulder because of an ironic twist of fate. Colombo has a World Trade Centre with twin towers. The buildings were attacked by terrorist vehicle bombs in 1996 and again in 1997. Although the 37-story towers were not knocked down there were hundreds of people wounded, many were killed. The Tamil Tigers were credited with the violence.

The Tamils represent 18 percent of the population, their leaders said they wanted autonomy, Sri Lankan politicians didn't think that was a good idea—they fought, no one won. Following al-Qaeda's destructive attack on America's twin towers, the United States designated the Tamil Tigers, among other violent organizations, as international terrorists. Sri Lankans were tired of fighting and the Tigers found world opinion swinging against them. Both sides embraced a cease fire agreement to negotiate their differences without violence. The Tamils speak Tamil, the Sinhalese make up 74 percent of the population and they speak Sinhala. Everyone also speaks English; literacy is high at 86 percent.

The refurbished twin towers in Colombo are the tallest buildings in a modest skyline; tourism is the highest it has been in 33 years.

I let my belt out another notch as my trip pleasantly revolved around food. There was lunch at the ornate Grand Oriental Hotel, a British barracks built in 1837, but converted to a hotel in 1875; lunch at the Lavinia Hotel, a hostel on the Indian Ocean built in 1805; and on another day, lunch at the Royal Colombo Golf Club, founded in 1875 to become the third oldest golf club in the world The course contains water hazards, crows that steal golf balls, and the Kelani Valley railroad crosses the course Once a golfer accidentally hit his ball into the engine's windshield, breaking it. The engineer stopped the train on the golf course and chased the golfer down for compensation on the broken glass.

People in Sri Lanka love and respect heritage whether it has to do with their family histories or evolution of their society. They pride themselves on the beautiful old buildings and the stories of adventure and struggle that go along with their landmarks and ancestry.

Of course, best for me was visiting children. There was a brief visit to the Christian Missionary College, a girl's school for grades K-12. Young Maleena Awn, 10, was in a program with classmates that centered on all things Chinese. The thirty 6th graders used their ingenuity to look Chinese; each had done research and could explain some aspect of Chinese culture. I met teachers and the principal; they were all purposeful, pleasant and a credit to their profession.

For many years, Sri Lanka was on the edge. No one knew whether the country would survive. Things are different now, there's optimism: people are laughing at silly things, kids are dressing up like the Chinese, crows are flying off with golf balls, the surf keeps plashing on pretty beaches, and there's a pleasant sunrise every morning—all good reasons to feel enriched by visiting Sri Lanka.

Bonjour in the South Pacific

Bonjour is the greeting one passes to another on the French island of Nouvelle Caledonie—in English the place is called New Caledonia.

As my good fortune continues in having an employer who believes travel should be my middle name, I recently spent several days a Noumea, the capital city. This is an area of the world where women wore grass skirts and men were cannibals. That was before work by British and French missionaries and colonization by soldiers and ex-convicts from France.

Today, New Caledonia is blessed with a temperate tropical climate, mountains, beaches, and 200,000 people of European, Polynesian, and Asian descent. There are also 135,000 cattle, and 110,000 tourists visiting annually from France, Japan, Australia, and New Zealand. Some of the tourists like to hang out in kava houses, shadowy cafes that serve kava, a beverage that pleasantly calms people down.

Caledonians love Americans. That affection stems from 1942 when 16,000 US troops established a base at Noumea that blocked invasion by the Japanese. In the city center there is an impressive red, white and blue memorial that honors America.

The small island nation also boosts the world's second largest natural reef and second largest nickel deposits. Best of all is the motivated, positive people that live there. I know this is to be true because I saw throngs of men, women and children happily jogging, walking, and bicycling along Noumea's waterside park. Up and down hillsides, the park is naturally landscaped and neatly maintained for miles along brick and dirt paths. Several days at both dusk and sunrise, I ran this trail huffing and puffing along with the French.

Once as two young women powered past me, I said a little too loud in English, *You're making the men look bad!* One of the women burst out in laughter as she explained in French to her running mate what I had said, then they both giggled as they surged ahead continuing to make men look bad.

In many places people are content to watch life's parade pass them by, my feeling is that those who live in Noumea are the parade and everyone is involved. While the northern hemisphere now enjoys summer, New Caledonia is in the southern hemisphere and is experiencing winter. With temperatures in the 60s, low humidity, purple-apricot sunsets on royal blue waters, people seldom find more perfect circumstances for enjoyment of outdoor fitness.

I've been thinking about American solipsism since we were led through our national exercise in patriotism preparing for the Iraqi War. My mental juices cooked as I received a ton of spam degrading the French as ungrateful cowards who had forgotten all the great things Americans had down for them. They were also accused of being old fashioned and out-of-touch with reality because they would not support armed conflict in Iraq. They preferred negotiation to violent confrontation, so did Canada, Germany, Russia, and most other countries in the world. The comments against the French weren't fair. Most of the disrespectful remarks were from people who weren't knowledgeable about the world and who forgets what.

Of course, the French are not cowards any more than Americans are cowards, nor have they forgotten our sacrifices in liberating their grandparents and parents. Who could forget that? Certainly the French people will not forget, that's something you don't lose sight of just as Americans will never forget that Benjamin Franklin was allowed to liberate a large portion of France's national treasury to finance the American Revolution. Without those millions of Francs that bought war materials, paid soldiers and built ships, the Revolution would have been short lived and today we'd be enjoying a spot of tea, snacking on fish and chips, and watching the telly.

On one of my evenings at Noumea, I had the unique opportunity for a gastronomical adventure with colleagues from France's Army and Navy. We spent several enjoyable hours flirting with French cuisine, sipping wine and swapping stories. Boys will be boys regardless of nationality. My most enjoyable stories were about Benjamin Franklin's life in Paris, his raid on the French treasury; and Lafayette's loyalty to George Washington and America's quest for liberty.

In one of the evening's most dramatic moments, French Lieutenant Colonel Bernard Lavel slapped his forehead as he recollected with great good humor that as a schoolboy his shock at learning the French had sold the Louisiana Purchase to the United States for a paltry $15 million. I laughed with the enjoyment that Thomas Jefferson must have felt over American's bargain. Acquired 200 years ago, the new territory more than doubled the size of the United States.

Everyone had at least one best French-American story of historical events. The evening was an exquisite boy's night out instruction into who remembers what. I am glad to report that no one has forgotten anything! Merci for reading along.

Holiday Spirit in Singapore

Is it me or have the past few weeks been more joyful than usual?" Let's see. I spent a week in Northern Thailand riding elephants, took a bamboo raft ride on the Ping River, visited peaceful Buddhist temples, saw my first butterfly park and a factory that makes paper from elephant dung, strolled through an orchid farm, met hill tribe people, walked around the lengthy city moat at Chiang Mai, called on giant pandas Kam-Ay and Kam-Aeu at the Chiang Mai Zoo, rode a train across the Thai countryside for 15 hours, and at Lopburi saw a thousand monkeys who live in the middle of town. It was my vacation.

I under-exercised, overslept, let another notch out on my belt, and didn't check e-mail. This is what I really saw: people looking prosperous because they were happy. I know that because they are calm, considerate, smile, and are friendly—all ingredients for a glad heart. None of this is an act, the residents of Northern Thailand are genuine and I was transformed in their presence.

Returning to Singapore, I found the landscape, along Orchard Road where I live, had added color and music to the holiday scene. Garland with bright red, blue, and green lights was wrapped around light poles, garland and lights strung across streets, and strings of white lights, probably millions of them are hanging from massive tropical trees. Walt Disney would look at the dazzling scene in wonder. The theme is *Christmas in the Tropics*, and there are larger-than-life red wooden soldiers guarding street corners, bell-shaped light sculptures, and artificial replicas of snowmen that don't feel threatened by warm temperatures. Stores have a crush of shoppers, popular holiday music, 30-50 foot Christmas trees with all the trimmings, and you can occasionally hear a little boy or girl singing, *...here comes Santa Claus, here comes Santa Claus, right down Santa Claus lane.* It is 88 degrees during the day,

75 degrees at night, we're not going to have a white Christmas, but it is the rainy season, there are cloudy skies and occasional tropical downpours.

A few days ago, I took a turn standing by a Salvation Army red kettle in front of Lucky Plaza, one of the neighborhood shopping malls. I rang a little bell that signaled *please donate to help the needy, please help!* Many people responded, one was a young Chinese woman with two pretty braids down her back. She slowly went through her small purse, finding some coins; she dropped them into the kettle. Watching her, I had a sense that she didn't have a lot, but whatever there was she would gladly share with strangers. After depositing her donation, she surprisingly took both my hands into hers; with a beautiful smile and through a serious speech impediment, she said, *Merry Christmas.* There are some moments in life that take your breath.

The next day, I passed a small store near where I work at Sembawang Wharves. In the window was a lovely artificial cherry tree with bright red blossoms. Hung on the tree were Chinese ornaments. I thought that it would be the perfect Christmas tree for me—simple, elegant, and colorful.

Entering the store, the owner approached and I asked about the tree. She said that she had it made and had been using it in her window since the last Chinese New Year. She also emphasized that she loved it. As I asked if it were for sale my vision of the perfect Christmas tree was fading. However, she said, *It is so interesting that you would stop by because I've been thinking of finding a good home for the tree.*

I probably sounded a little too eager when I responded, *I have a good home...if you were to sell the tree, how much would it cost?*

She said: *Oh, no, no, I could not take money, I must give it.*

This was one of those times when an improbable situation was presenting itself. What do you do? Well, if you're me, you agree to a free tree and the owner's offer of free delivery. It does little good to argue with grace, it's just best to standby until circumstances allow you to show a stranger the quality of your own generous spirit.

The following day, I stopped by to see Lai Li Lian for a treatment in foot reflexology. Li Lian is one of those talented people who know how to stimulate a jogger's feet. She has strong hands that massage reflex points in making the whole body feel better. Li Lian is a Buddhist who chants on Sundays, does yoga every day, and meditates often. Still she complains that she must work harder to be a better Buddhist. One reason for her sense of failure is that she recently killed a pesky mosquito. I didn't laugh, she was serious.

At any rate, following the foot treatment, I mentioned that my nails were a little ragged; Li Lian promptly gave me a manicure that is as in free manicure. She would not accept payment. That's holiday spirit for you!

So is life a little more joyful this time of year? Obviously I don't often vacation in Northern Thailand or seemingly become the recipient of as much goodwill from strangers; however, there are no days that pass in which people do not extend themselves in one way or another to make my life better. Courtesy and respect create a foundation for relationships that flourish. I reciprocate and often initiate the interaction. All of us do our part, we try to make the lives of those around us a little better and when we're successful, we find our own lives improved in the process. At holidays like Christmas when our spirit of brotherhood and sisterhood is brought closer to the heart, the difference that people make in our lives seems more powerful. But just as often it is the same generous spirit that surrounds us at every other time of the year, we simply notice it more.

Farewell Kimmy

On December 30, I received a note from Diane Mathis in Washington, DC. Diane wrote: *It is with the heaviest of heart that I inform you that our beloved Kimberly passed away yesterday, December 29, 2003, at 8:42 am at Holy Cross Hospital. She fought a hard battle against a cruel monster. She is at rest now. Her mom's address is Hannah Henry, 12005 Eaglewood Court, Silver Spring, Maryland 20202-1873.*

So many times when someone from the human family leaves us we overstate the goodness that that individuals brought to their family, friends and strangers. That wouldn't be possible with Kim Henry. She possessed one of the most giving and loving hearts of anyone I've met, was a strong advocate for the homeless and needy, and was an especially hard fighter for breast cancer long before she contracted the disease herself.

Kim used her public speaking skills developed as a member of Toastmasters International to become a leader and spokeswoman for breast cancer awareness. She was a strong advocate for The Susan G. Komen Breast Cancer Foundation. As a testimonial to her impact on those around her, her coworkers at the Military Sealift Command who voluntarily donated at least six months of their vacation days to keep Kim on the US Navy payroll throughout her lengthy hospitalization. Kim was an only child, her father passed away before she was born, her mother is now alone with a loss that would appear inconsolable, but let's please try with our notes and prayers.

Acknowledgements

I am more fortunate than most because of the high quality of my journey. The 96 vignettes in *The Human Condition* are a reflection on the good people whose paths have crossed mine.

These small stories are from experiences in 1998 through 2003. At first living in Northern Virginia and working for the Naval Criminal Investigative Service, I was drawn to volunteerism with spare time devoted to helping raise awareness and funds for breast cancer research, treatment, and prevention; feeding the homeless, running marathons for good causes, and helping myself and other people find themselves through Toastmasters International.

In the sphere of breast cancer, The Honorable Nancy Brinker, founder of The Susan G. Komen Breast Cancer Foundation and former Ambassador to Hungary, has been and continues to be a huge inspiration. Her example of selflessness and high energy to improve women's health has inspiring thousands of followers, me included. Since initially being recruited in the corps of volunteers benefiting The Komen Foundation, I have become a better man through knowing the following survivors: Vickie Martin Adamson, Ernestine Ashley, Connie Bash, Patti Brownstein, Amy Cruz (now deceased), Roberta Culp (now deceased), Nancy Fosbrook, Kelly Gallagher, Kim Henry (now deceased), Vivian Hines (now deceased), Di Keith Jones, Rana Kahl, Judy Macon, Kathy Mills, Ada Palmer, Judy Pickett, Susan Shinderman, Susan Sonley, Beth Swanson, Gwen Talbot, Donna Weston, and Kim Wright.

From the onset of my participation with Toastmasters International there have been literally hundreds of people who touched my heart with their words. The most memorable has been Pauline Shirley, past president of Toastmasters International, good friend to everyone, and shining example of how we should all use our personalities to reach out to others. I have met literally thousands of Toastmasters, people with strong personalities and mostly good ideas about living a more meaningful life. Some that come to mind are Cindy Alvarez, Darby Jo Arakelian, Roger Baker, John Barnish Joyce Battle, <u>Karen Booker,</u> Eve Cameron, Faye Carroll, Kellie Carroll, Christine Cawayan, Ernest Chen, Peter Colwell, Ralph Compton, Jo Condrill, James Duncan, Paula Emerick, Fred Ferate, Ann Ferrante, Tony Gaston, Fran Gedra, Carol Harris, Frank Huffman, John and Barbara Hunt, Michelle James, Loretta Johnson, Renee Jones, Cindy Juvan, Joann Koos, Ginny Kibler, Tammy Kukla, Nelson Latona, Martha Lee, Rebekah Lee, Ron Leo, Brooks and Dina Loomis, Diane Mathis, Shirley Mattingly, Marianne Meadows, Darric Milligan, Shelley Mitchell, William Moore, Ben Pina, Kay Presto, Gayla Reilly, Kim Roman, Amy Ryan, Mike and Linda Schultz, George Scott, Joan Thomas, Geri Wallace, Bill Webster, David Woodhouse, and Nisa Wichitsiri.

In my career with the Naval Criminal Investigative Service I was lucky in traveling to Asia, Europe and the United States as part of my work. In the combination of all these experiences I learned that truly the more we give the more we get in return. My most heartfelt thanks to my former supervisor, Les Vay, who generously provided me job enrichment in these traveling opportunities and selecting me for a four year assignment in Singapore. A US Marine Officer, federal civilian employee, and now a retiree, Les was a pacesetter in fair-mindedness and continues to be a wonderful gentleman and friend.

In my official travels I was seldom by myself. There was usually at least one stalwart workmate that kept me focused on the work at hand, shared their good humor and gave generously from a gift for gab. Personalities that come to mind are Scott Bernat, Bob Blons, Tom Boungivino, Frank Boyd, Joe Brummond, Mike Bryant, Jim Campbell, Brian Curley, Mike Douglas, Lane Ford, Kel Ide, Jeri Jones, Nate Knowles, Michelle Kramer, Chris Leaden, Dennis Manning, Rich McFetrich, Chris Neal, Alma Peterson, Corbin Rinehart, Pia Roth, John Salazar, John Smallman, Angelo Tjoumas, and Kevin Wagoner. My travel stories are from our shared experiences.

Moving around the world isn't easy; my journey has been less strenuous because of strong friendships that gave me the right kind of orientation. I am indebted to the following generous and knowledgeable personalities who taught me the rights and wrongs of life in their world: Frank Bennett, England; Kemariah Duraman, Brunei; Hyacinth Dmello, Bruno D'Souza, George Martin, Jahangir and Merion Telyarkhan, Keki Master, and Lonny Fernandes and son Hayston, India; Julie Ambarsari, Kristin Febrianti Caroline, Tom Daley, Lucky Santini, Netty Kacaribu, Ginny Rustandi, Budi Setyaning, Dewi "Shanty" Susantini Luh, Inggrids Lubis Collyns, and Kusrini "Rina" Endang Sri, Indonesia; Bruce Acker, Bob Tate and Phoebe Chan, Malaysia; Walter Etcheverry, Roger Girard and Bernard Lavel, New Caledonia; Felicia Fernandes and Jim Roberts, East Timor; Lemapu Wong, Samoa; Terry and Nora Leggett, Doris Bay, Captain Annie Lim, Lai Li Lian, Dr. Robert Don, Shila Mohammed, and Ernest Chen, Singapore; Majid and Leena Awn and family, Jim Oxley, and Tee Sims, Sri Lanka; Supaporn Toluang and son Copter, Wanvisa Techo and family, Chamaiporn "Lek" Sompinta, Eiw Boontiwa and daughter Jubjang, Thamnian "Elle" Tool-ong, Dokrang "Frean" Traiking, and Tantimaphon "Emm" Jaichuen, Thailand; Andrew Manuele, Vanuatu; and Tran Thi Mong Chinh, Nguyen Thi Hong Van, Pham Choung Dai, Robb Etnyre, and John Milkiewicz, Vietnam.

Thank you to my peer readers and reviewers: Jean Bird Spike, Ernest Chen, Anna Tjoumas, Karen Edwards and Ivory Chang. More than peers, they are kind friends and that shows in their encouragement for others to read this book.

Thanks to the strangers who became friends, the hundreds of people who looked out for my well being, and all those who cared enough to share something about their lives. Each time I was touched by these human hands I was educated and entertained, having my heart expanded in the process.

I've tried to demonstrate through these reflections that although we are obviously different in skin color, religious beliefs, economic circumstances, thinking patterns, and culture, we're all closely related in the human family. We share commonality in our good hearts and the love we contribute to those around us.

I am indebted to friends, family and strangers who have kept me smiling and wondering, made me rich in experiences, and taught me the value of positive thinking. Indeed, everyone we meet is our teacher to contribute another piece to the complicated puzzle that comprises the human condition.

Lastly, thank you to my dad, Larry Welch, Sr., for everything. The best thing about my dad was that he was a lovely man--kind-hearted, smiling, and loyal to his family. He was a model son to his parents, gave unstintingly to those around him, and was a monument of support to my sisters and me. No days pass that we don't think good thoughts of him.

Cover Design

Muslim children at village of Pasinani, Java, Indonesia, 2007

Design and photograph by Larry Welch.

Index

Printed in the United States
By Bookmasters